The World of Functions

Families of Functions and the Algebra of Functions

Teacher's Guide

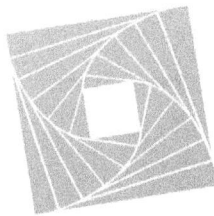

This material is based upon work supported by the National Science Foundation under award numbers ESI-9255262, ESI-0137805, and ESI-0627821. Any opinions, findings, and conclusions or recommendations expressed in this publication are those of the authors and do not necessarily reflect the views of the National Science Foundation.

Key Curriculum
1150 65th Street
Emeryville, California 94608
email: editorial@keypress.com
www.keycurriculum.com

First Edition Authors

Dan Fendel, Diane Resek, Lynne Alper, and Sherry Fraser

Contributors to the Second Edition

Sherry Fraser, Jean Klanica, Brian Lawler, Eric Robinson, Lew Romagnano, Rick Marks, Dan Brutlag, Alan Olds, Mike Bryant, Jeri P. Philbrick, Lori Green, Matt Bremer, Margaret DeArmond

Editor

Mali Apple

Editorial Assistant

Emily Reed

Professional Reviewer

Rick Marks, Sonoma State University

Math Checker

Carrie Gongaware

Production Editor

Andrew Jones

Production Director

Christine Osborne

Executive Editor

Josephine Noah

Mathematics Product Manager

Elizabeth DeCarli

Publisher

Steven Rasmussen

Contents

Blackline Masters

Calculator Guide and Calculator Notes

Introduction

The World of Functions Unit Overview

Intent

In this unit, students explore many concepts related to functions, including combining functions, composing functions, and transforming functions.

Mathematics

Over the course of this unit, students develop a wide range of ideas about functions. The main concepts and skills that students will encounter and practice during the unit are summarized below.

General Notions Regarding Functions
- Recognizing four ways of representing a function—tabular, graphical, algebraic, and situational—and moving from one representation to another
- Formally defining functions as sets of ordered pairs
- Reviewing some basic families of functions

Properties of Specific Families of Functions
- Finding, describing, and proving patterns in the tables of linear, quadratic, cubic, and exponential functions based on the algebraic form of the functions
- Seeing the sets of linear and exponential functions as two-parameter families and comparing the two types of growth
- Applying the concepts of direct and inverse proportionality and constants of proportionality
- Using absolute value functions and step functions to model problem situations
- Using rational functions to model problem situations

End Behavior and Asymptotes of Functions
- Finding vertical and horizontal asymptotes for specific functions and finding functions with given asymptotes
- Relating asymptotic behavior to situations
- Characterizing end behavior of functions and finding the behavior of particular functions

Fitting Functions to Data
- Finding the specific function in a given family to fit a given situation or set of data
- Developing a measure of "quality of fit" of a function to a set of data
- Applying the least-squares criterion for quality of fit

- Using a calculator's regression feature to find a function that fits a given set of data

Combining and Modifying Functions
- Arithmetic operations on functions
  - Describing situations using arithmetic combinations of functions
  - Relating arithmetic operations on functions to graphs
  - Formally defining arithmetic operations on functions
- Composition of Functions
  - Developing the concept of composition of functions based on situations
  - Defining composition notation
  - Establishing that composition is not commutative
  - Composing and decomposing functions
- Inverse functions
  - Formally defining the concept of inverse function
  - Finding a general algebraic equation for the inverse of a linear function
  - Relating the concept of inverse function to graphs, tables, and situations
  - Seeing that the graph of an inverse function is a reflection of the graph of the original function
- Transformations of functions
  - Finding the graphs and tables of transformations of functions
  - Using functional notation and understanding its use in characterizing the transformations of functions

Progression

The unit builds on students' previous work with functions. A major element of the unit is the exploration of families of functions from four major perspectives: as tables, as graphs, as equations, and as models for real-world situations. Over the course of the unit, students explore many basic families of functions, including linear, quadratic, cubic, general polynomial, exponential, sine, logarithmic, reciprocal, and rational functions.

Students' exploration of tables includes algebraic proofs showing that linear functions have constant differences and that quadratic functions have constant second differences (based on regularly increasing inputs). Their study of graphs includes work with vertical and horizontal asymptotes. They also study the idea of a "least squares" approximation of a function using a set of data points (from a graph or table) and learn to find functions that fit specific data using the regression feature of their calculators.

Students' work with functions to represent real-world situations includes the task of finding a specific function in a given family to model a particular problem. They learn that finding an appropriate function to use as a model sometimes involves recognizing a pattern in the data and other times requires insight into the situation itself.

Later in the unit, students explore ways of combining functions, using arithmetic operations and composition, and see how these operations are related to algebraic representations, graphs, tables, and situations. The work with composition includes the concept of inverse function and its connection to graphs and tables.

Students conclude the unit by returning to a richer version of the opening problem, *Brake!* They use the knowledge and insight they have gained about functions to find a function that fits the new information.

The What and Why of Functions: Formally defining the concept of a function; discussing different representations of functions and the usefulness of functions

Tables: Looking for patterns in the tables of linear, quadratic, cubic, and exponential functions, and proving the patterns

Going to the Limit: Learning about asymptotes and other end behavior of functions

Who's Who?: Locating the particular member of a function family that fits a situation once one knows to which family the function belongs

A Tight Fit: Exploring the meaning of "best fit" and using the calculator's regression feature

Back to Arithmetic: Creating new functions using arithmetic operations and examining the effect in terms of the four perspectives on functions

Composing Functions: Examining composition of functions in terms of the four perspectives on functions; formally defining inverse functions in terms of composition

Transforming Functions: Studying transformation of functions in terms of the four perspectives on functions

Back to the Beginning: Returning to a more realistic version of the activity *Brake!*

Pacing Guides

50-minute Pacing Guide (32 days)

Day	Activity	In-Class Time Estimate
1	The What and Why of Functions	0
	Brake!	45
	Introduce: POW 2: One Mile at a Time	5
	Homework: Story Sketches	0
2	Brake! (continued)	15
	Discussion: Story Sketches	35
	Homework: Story Sketches II	0
3	Discussion: Story Sketches II	20
	What Good Are Functions?	30
	Homework: More Families	0
4	Discussion: More Families	15
	Tables	0
	Linear Tables	35
	Homework: Story Sketches III	0
5	Discussion: Story Sketches III	10
	Quadratic Tables	40
	Homework: Back to the Basics	0
6	Discussion: Back to the Basics	15
	Quadratic Tables by Algebra	35
	Homework: A General Quadratic	0
7	Discussion: A General Quadratic	15
	Exponential Tables	35
	Homework: A Cubic Pattern	0
8	Presentations: POW 2: One Mile at a Time	15
	Exponential Tables (continued)	15
	Discussion: A Cubic Pattern	10
	Introduce: POW 3: A Spin on Transitivity	10
	Homework: Mystery Tables	0
9	Discussion: Mystery Tables	10
	"Brake!" Revisited	35

	Homework: Bigger Means Smaller	5
10	Going to the Limit	0
	Discussion: Bigger Means Smaller	10
	Don't Divide That!	40
	Homework: Difficult Denominators	0
11	Discussion: Difficult Denominators	10
	Return of the Shadow	40
	Homework: An Average Drive	0
12	Discussion: An Average Drive	20
	Approaching Infinity	5
	The End of the Function	25
	Homework: Creating the Ending You Want	0
13	Discussion: Creating the Ending You Want	10
	The End of the Function (continued)	15
	Who's Who?	0
	Families Have Many Different Members	25
	Homework: Fitting Mia's Birdhouses Again	0
14	Discussion: Fitting Mia's Birdhouses Again	15
	Families Have Many Different Members (continued)	35
	Homework: Mystery Tables II	0
15	Discussion: Mystery Tables II	10
	What Will It Be Worth?	40
	Homework: The Decision About Dunkalot	0
16	A Tight Fit	0
	Discussion: The Decision About Dunkalot	30
	Let's Regress	20
	Homework: Midnight Express	0
17	Presentations: POW 3: A Spin on Transitivity	15
	Discussion: Midnight Express	15
	Let's Regress (continued)	10
	Introduce: POW 4: It's Off to College We Go	10
	Homework: In the Lead	0
18	Discussion: In the Lead	20
	Back to Arithmetic	0
	The Arithmetic of Functions	25

	Homework: The Arithmetic of Graphs	5
19	Discussion: The Arithmetic of Graphs	15
	Back to the Corral	35
	Homework: Name That Family!	0
20	Discussion: Name That Family!	20
	Back to the Corral (continued)	30
	Homework: "Small World, Isn't It?" Revisited	0
21	Discussion: "Small World, Isn't It?" Revisited	10
	Composing Functions	0
	Rumble, Grumble	40
	Homework: The Composition of Functions	0
22	Discussion: The Composition of Functions	20
	The Cost of Pollution	30
	Homework: Order Among the Functions	0
23	Discussion: Order Among the Functions	20
	The Cost of Pollution (continued)	30
	Homework: Cozying Up to Composition	0
24	Discussion: Cozying Up to Composition	15
	Taking Functions Apart	35
	Homework: Fish, Ladders, and Bacteria	0
25	Discussion: Fish, Ladders, and Bacteria	25
	Functions in Verse	25
	Homework: Linear Functions in Verse	0
26	Discussion: Linear Functions in Verse	15
	Functions in Verse (continued)	25
	Homework: An Inventory of Inverses	10
27	Discussion: An Inventory of Inverses	15
	Transforming Functions	0
	Double Dose of Functions	35
	Homework: Slide That Function	0
28	Discussion: Slide That Function	20
	Discussion: POW 4: It's Off to College We Go	30
	Homework: Transforming Graphs, Tables, and Situations	0
29	Discussion: Transforming Graphs, Tables, and Situations	20

	Back to the Beginning	0
	Better Braking	30
	Homework: Beginning Portfolio Selection	0
30	Discussion: Beginning Portfolio Selection	10
	Better Braking (continued)	40
	Homework: "The World of Functions" Portfolio	0
31	In-Class Assessment	45
	Homework: Take-Home Assessment	5
32	Exam Discussion	35
	Unit Reflection	15

90-minute Pacing Guide (22 days)

Day	Activity	In-Class Time Estimate
1	The What and Why of Functions	0
	Brake!	55
	Introduce: *POW 2: One Mile at a Time*	10
	Story Sketches	25
	Homework: *Story Sketches II*	0
2	*Story Sketches* (continued)	35
	Discussion: *Story Sketches II*	20
	What Good Are Functions?	35
	Homework: *More Families*	0
3	Discussion: *More Families*	15
	Tables	0
	Linear Tables	35
	Quadratic Tables	40
	Homework: *Story Sketches III*	0
4	Discussion: *Story Sketches III*	10
	Back to the Basics	45
	Quadratic Tables by Algebra	35
	Homework: *A General Quadratic*	0
5	Discussion: *A General Quadratic*	25
	Exponential Tables	65
	Homework: *A Cubic Pattern*	0
6	Presentations: *POW 2: One Mile at a Time*	15
	Introduce: *POW 3: A Spin on Transitivity*	10
	Discussion: *A Cubic Pattern*	15
	Mystery Tables	50
	Homework: *"Brake!" Revisited*	0
7	Discussion: *"Brake!" Revisited*	15
	Bigger Means Smaller	35
	Going to the Limit	0

	Don't Divide That!	40
	Homework: *Difficult Denominators*	0
8	Discussion: *Difficult Denominators*	10
	Return of the Shadow	35
	An Average Drive	40
	Approaching Infinity	5
	Homework: *The End of the Function*	0
9	Discussion: *The End of the Function*	20
	Creating the Ending You Want	40
	Who's Who?	0
	Families Have Many Different Members	30
	Homework: *Fitting Mia's Birdhouses Again*	0
10	Discussion: *Fitting Mia's Birdhouses Again*	15
	Families Have Many Different Members (continued)	35
	What Will It Be Worth?	40
	Homework: *Mystery Tables II*	0
11	Discussion: *Mystery Tables II*	15
	The Decision About Dunkalot	55
	A Tight Fit	0
	Let's Regress	20
	Homework: *Midnight Express*	0
12	Presentations: *POW 3: A Spin on Transitivity*	15
	Introduce: *POW 4: It's Off to College We Go*	5
	Discussion: *Midnight Express*	15
	Let's Regress (continued)	10
	In the Lead	40
	Back to Arithmetic	0
	Homework: *The Arithmetic of Functions*	5
13	Discussion: *The Arithmetic of Functions*	5
	The Arithmetic of Graphs	50
	Back to the Corral	35
	Homework: *Name That Family!*	0
14	Discussion: *Name That Family!*	20

	Back to the Corral (continued)	30
	"Small World, Isn't It?" Revisited	40
	Composing Functions	0
	Homework: *Rumble, Grumble*	0
15	Discussion: *Rumble, Grumble*	15
	The Composition of Functions	45
	The Cost of Pollution	30
	Homework: *Order Among the Functions*	0
16	Discussion: *Order Among the Functions*	20
	The Cost of Pollution (continued)	25
	Cozying Up to Composition	45
	Homework: *Taking Functions Apart*	0
17	Discussion: *Taking Functions Apart*	10
	Fish, Ladders, and Bacteria	55
	Functions in Verse	25
	Homework: *Linear Functions in Verse*	0
18	Discussion: *Linear Functions in Verse*	10
	Functions in Verse (continued)	25
	An Inventory of Inverses	55
	Transforming Functions	0
	Homework: *Double Dose of Functions*	0
19	Discussion: *POW 4: It's Off to College We Go*	30
	Discussion: *Double Dose of Functions*	10
	Slide That Function	50
	Homework: *Transforming Graphs, Tables, and Situations*	0
20	Discussion: *Transforming Graphs, Tables, and Situations*	20
	Back to the Beginning	0
	Better Braking	70
	Homework: *Beginning Portfolio Selection* and *"The World of Functions"* Portfolio	0
21	Discussion: *Beginning Portfolio Selection* and *"The World of Functions"* Portfolio	10
	In-Class Assessment	45
	Homework: Take-Home Assessment (begin in class)	35

Materials and Supplies

All IMP classrooms should have a set of standard supplies, described in the section "Materials and Supplies for the IMP Classroom" in *A Guide to IMP.* You'll also find a comprehensive list of materials needed for all Year 4 units in the section "Materials and Supplies for Year 4" in the *Year 4 Teacher's Guide* general resources.

Listed here are the supplies needed for this unit. Also available are general and activity-specific blackline masters, for transparencies or for student worksheets, in the "Blackline Masters" section in *The World of Functions* Unit Resources.

The World of Functions Materials

Optional: Firm rubber ball or golf ball (to demonstrate exponential decay)
IMP student books from Years 1 to 3
Optional: Students' portfolios for Years 1 to 3

More About Supplies

Graph paper is a standard supply for IMP classrooms. Blackline masters of 1-Centimeter Graph Paper, ¼-Inch Graph Paper, and 1-Inch Graph Paper are provided, for you to make copies and transparencies.

Assessing Progress

The World of Functions concludes with two formal unit assessments. In addition, there are many opportunities for more informal, ongoing assessments throughout the unit. For more information about assessment and grading, including general information about the end-of-unit assessments and how to use them, consult *A Guide to IMP*.

End-of-Unit Assessments

This unit concludes with in-class and take-home assessments. The in-class assessment is intentionally short so that time pressures will not affect student performance. Students may use graphing calculators and their notes from previous work when they take the assessments. You can download unit assessments from the *The World of Functions* Unit Resources.

Ongoing Assessment

One of the primary tasks of the classroom teacher is to assess student learning. Although the assigning of course grades may be part of this process, assessment more broadly includes the daily work of determining how well students understand key ideas and what level of achievement they have attained on key skills, in order to provide the best possible ongoing instructional program for them.

Students' written and oral work provides many opportunities for teachers to gather this information. We make some recommendations here of activities to monitor especially carefully that will give you insight into student progress.

- *What Good Are Functions?*
- *Exponential Tables*
- *Families Have Many Different Members*
- *Name That Family!*
- *The Cost of Pollution*
- *Better Braking*

Discussion of Unit Assessments

Have students volunteer to explain their work on each of the problems. Encourage questions and alternate explanations from other students.

In-Class Assessment

The functions can all be expressed by fairly simple equations:

$$f(x) = 20x$$
$$g(x) = 2^{x/2}$$
$$h(x) = 5x^2$$
$$k(x) = \frac{1}{2x}$$

Take-Home Assessment

For Part I, you might begin by having students match up the situations with the graphs, and then discuss the function family in each case.

- *Situation a:* This is a cubic function and goes with graph Z.
- *Situation b:* This is a rational or "reciprocal" function and goes with graph X.
- *Situation c:* This is a sine family function and goes with graph U.
- *Situation d*: This situation goes with graph W. The graph is a hyperbola (see discussion of Question 1 of *Story Sketches III*), but students may not be able to identify the family in this case. They may think the graph is a parabola, in which case the function would be in the quadratic family. Although this is not correct, the situation can be represented by a quadratic *equation,* involving both d^2 and t^2, so such thinking would not be far off.

Graph V is a linear function, and graph Y is a quadratic function. These graphs do not fit any of the situations.

For Part II, have a few volunteers explain some sample entries in the tables. You probably will not need to go over all of the entries. Here is the complete table (using estimates from the graph of *f*):

x	(f + g)(x)	(f ∘ g)(x)	f(x + 2)	2g(x) + 1
−5	5.2	−3.3	2.8	7
−3	10.7	−1.4	1.8	17
1	−3.9	2.7	−3.3	−3
3	−1.3	−2.8	−3.2	5
5	5.7	−0.4	−2.0	19

Supplemental Activities

The unit contains a variety of activities at the end of the student pages that you can use to supplement the regular unit material. These activities fall roughly into two categories.

Reinforcements increase students' understanding and comfort with concepts, techniques, and methods that are discussed in class and are central to the unit.

Extensions allow students to explore ideas beyond those presented in the unit, including generalizations and abstractions of ideas.

The supplemental activities are presented in the teacher's guide and the student book in the approximate sequence in which you might use them. Below are specific recommendations about how each activity might work within the unit. You may wish to use some of these activities, especially the later ones, after the unit is completed.

***From Second Differences to Quadratics* (extension)** In *Quadratic Tables*, students see that the tables of quadratic functions have constant second differences (when inputs are equally spaced). This supplemental activity looks at a partial converse. It asks students to prove that if a function has constant second differences for any table that uses consecutive integer inputs, then, at least for integer inputs, the function is quadratic. This activity can be used following the discussion of *A General Quadratic*.

***Real Domains* (extension)** Because the discussion of asymptotes is a natural lead-in to the issue of domains, this activity is appropriate for use after *Creating the Ending You Want*.

***Absolutely Functions* (extension or reinforcement)** This activity can serve as a follow-up to *Midnight Express,* as Question 1 of that activity involves an absolute value expression.

***Odd or Even?* (extension)** The concept of odd and even functions is fairly abstract and might be introduced toward the end of the unit, perhaps after *The Arithmetic of Functions*.

***Graphing Power* (extension or reinforcement)** This activity works well following *Odd or Even?*, as students focus on properties of odd and even power functions.

***Ferris Wheel on a Ramp* and *Freddie on the Ferris Wheel* (extension or reinforcement)** These two activities involve sums of functions and might be used any time after *The Arithmetic of Functions*.

Over, and Over, and Over, and ... **(extension)** This activity continues students' work with composition of functions. It focuses on the composition of a function with itself and is a good follow-up to *Cozying Up to Composition*.

Its Own Inverse **(extension)** This activity can be used after *Linear Functions in Verse*.

A Hyperbolic Approach **(extension)** This activity is a follow-up to Question 1 of *Story Sketches III*. However, as Question 2 really involves transformation of functions, it is best assigned after *Transforming Graphs, Tables, and Situations*.

"Small World" Again! **(extension or reinforcement)** This activity makes a nice culmination of the unit. Students return to the population data set from the Year 3 unit *Small World, Isn't It?* and use their new knowledge to look for a function that gives a better fit to that data set.

The What and Why of Functions

Intent

In these activities, students recall what they know about functions and begin to classify functions into distinct families.

Mathematics

Students are reminded that functions can be viewed as relationships in situations, as algebraic expressions, as graphs, or as tables of values. The activities in *The What and Why of Functions* primarily focus on the first three representations, asking students to use descriptions of situations to develop algebraic expressions and sketches of graphs. Students see that the various functions they have developed and used throughout the IMP curriculum are representative of entire families of functions.

Progression

Brake! introduces the topic of functions and leads into a discussion of just what a function is. *Story Sketches* looks at the families of linear functions and exponential growth functions. *Story Sketches II* considers the families of sine functions and exponential decay functions, and *More Families* reviews the families of quadratic functions, cubic functions, power functions, and polynomial functions. *What Good Are Functions?* uses the context of prior IMP units to highlight the usefulness of functions in solving problems.

Brake!
POW 2: One Mile at a Time
Story Sketches
Story Sketches II
What Good Are Functions?
More Families

Brake!

Intent

This activity introduces the central unit theme.

Mathematics

Functions are the central topic of this unit, and this activity introduces that theme as students study a data set and try to describe what it tells them about the situation that produced the data. The discussion leading into this activity introduces the formal definition of a function and suggests that a function can be thought of in terms of a table of values, a graph, an equation or algorithm, or a relationship from a situation. The discussion also highlights vocabulary related to functions.

Progression

The teacher introduces this activity by explaining that the unit focuses on working with functions, not on a single central problem. Students do focused free-writing on the question, "What is a function?" After they share ideas, the teacher suggests four ways of looking at functions and helps students develop a formal definition of a function.

Students then work in groups to examine a table of data for a real-world situation. For now, they will represent this function as a graph, describe patterns in the data set, and use the data set to make a prediction. Students will return to this situation in *"Brake!" Revisited* to find an equation for this function. They will also examine a more complex version of the situation near the close of the unit, in *Better Braking.*

Approximate Time

45 to 55 minutes

Classroom Organization

Small groups, followed by whole-class discussion

Doing the Activity

Tell students that instead of having a central problem to solve, this unit will look at the concept of a function and at various ways to work with functions. To get students started, you might have them do focused free-writing on this question: **What is a function?** (Read about focused free-writing in "Student Communication: Oral and Written Presentation" in *A Guide to IMP.*)

Let students share ideas. As needed, add that mathematicians often identify four ways of looking at a function:
- As a table of values
- As a graph
- As an equation
- As a relationship between quantities in a real-world situation

A Formal Definition of Function

Tell students that mathematicians rely on both intuition and precise definitions. They define **function** formally in a way that is essentially like a table of values or a graph, namely, as a certain type of set of ordered pairs. You might begin to set up the formal definition as follows:

> **A function is a set of ordered pairs (or number pairs) that satisfies this condition: [definition to be completed in the discussion below].**

Before discussing what "this condition" refers to, ask, How is a set of ordered pairs like an In-Out table or a graph? Be sure students see that each ordered pair can represent either a row of a table or a point on a graph.

Review the fact that we often refer to the first component of an ordered pair as the *In* or *input* and to the second component as the *Out* or *output*. Also review that the variables representing these components are called the *independent* and *dependent* variables, respectively.

Then ask, What condition must the set of ordered pairs satisfy in order to be a function? Students have had some informal exposure to this idea. If they do not know, tell them that the condition is this:

> **There are no two ordered pairs with the same input and different outputs.**

Ask, What does this condition means in terms of the different ways of thinking about functions? As part of this exploration, ask students for examples that are not functions. What are some tables, graphs, or equations that do not represent functions? For instance, they should come up with tables in which the same input appears with different outputs or with graphs that violate the vertical-line test.

Students should reach these conclusions about the condition that makes a set of ordered pairs a function:
- With a table: The condition means that two rows of a table with the same *In* must have the same *Out* (or more simply, that there are never two rows with the same *In*).
- With a graph: Students should connect this condition with the vertical-line test.

- With a situation: Intuitively, a function describes how one thing "depends on" another. If the "causing factor" doesn't change, the result shouldn't either.

Also review the terms *domain* and *range.* Help students see that these terms can be defined along these lines:
- The **domain** of a function is the set of all numeric values that can occur as inputs.
- The **range** of a function is the set of all numeric values that can occur as outputs.

Two other general points are worth making:
- We often think of a function in terms of a "cause and effect" phenomenon, but this is not part of the formal definition. The input and output do not need to have any sort of causal relationship.
- We often think of functions in terms of equations, but this is also not part of the formal definition. Any set of pairs that fits the defining condition is a function, even if it can't be described by an equation.

You may also want to mention that the formal definition was developed over time, as mathematicians began to see the need to clarify what was and was not a function.

Tell students that after today's activity, they will begin to look at some basic families of functions, most of which they are already familiar with. Later in the unit, they will look at what happens when they combine functions in various ways.

Although the situation in this activity is revisited both in *"Brake" Revisited* and *Better Braking*, you may want to remind students that this is not a central unit problem as they have worked with in other units.

Discussing and Debriefing the Activity

When each group has decided on a prediction for 70 mph, begin the discussion, starting with one or two presentations of the graph. The class can talk about any questions that come up about choice of scales and so on.

Ask, Should the points on your graph be connected? What would it mean to connect them? In this case, the situation makes sense for speeds between those in the table, but the table does not state what the stopping distances should be. Presumably, some sort of smooth curve connecting the points will give correct values, but the only specific values students know are those in the table.

Have each group mention a pattern in the table, continuing until the class runs out of new patterns.

Next, discuss each group's prediction and explanation. Here are some of the approaches that might come up:

- A purely graphical estimate: Students may simply connect the data points with a smooth curve and then extend the curve.
- An estimate based on a pattern in the table: For example, students may have noticed that the stopping distance for 40 mph is exactly four times that for 20 mph and concluded that doubling the speed multiplies the stopping distance by 4. (This also fits the stopping distances for 25 mph and 50 mph.)

  Applying this pattern to 35 mph and 70 mph gives 4 · 68.0 = 272.0 feet as the stopping distance for 70 mph.

  Another pattern can be found by observing that the increases from row to row form a fairly regular pattern. Extending this pattern also gives 272 feet. (Students will explore this type of pattern further in *Quadratic Tables*.)
- An estimate found by substituting into an approximate algebraic equation: If any students found an equation for the table, have them explain how they found it. (If not, you need not take time to look for one now; students will do so in *"Brake!" Revisited*.)

Key Questions

How is a set of ordered pairs like an In-Out table or a graph?
What condition must the set of ordered pairs satisfy in order to be a function?
What does this condition, that no two ordered pairs with the same input have different outputs, mean in terms of the different ways of thinking about functions?
What are some tables, graphs, or equations that do not represent functions?
Should the points on your graph be connected? What would it mean to connect them?

POW 2: One Mile at a Time

Intent

Students use an algebraic representation of a problem situation to prove their solution is unique.

Mathematics

Students might solve the problem simply by guess-and-check. But the point of the POW is justifying the answer and writing a good argument that it is the only possible answer, based upon an algebraic approach.

Progression

Give students a week or more to work on this POW. Presentations will follow.

Approximate Time

5 to 10 minutes for introduction
2 to 3 hours for activity (at home)
15 minutes for presentations and discussion

Classroom Organization

Individuals, followed by whole-class presentations and discussion

Doing the Activity

To introduce the POW, you may want to talk about the problem situation that is presented. Clarify that the task involves more than just finding the answer to the problem.

On the day before the POW is due, select three students to make presentations on the following day. If you are aware of students who did this problem in different ways, select presenters accordingly.

Discussing and Debriefing the Activity

Have three students present their work. The problem can be approached in several ways, and proofs will depend on the methods chosen. Some students may have found the answer by guess-and-check. Others may have reasoned that the hundreds digit for the third milepost must be 1 and then built on that idea.

The main goal in this POW, however, is to express the problem algebraically and then use algebra to find and prove the answer. Toward that goal, ask, How can you represent a number with specific digits in terms of powers of 10?

For instance, if the number on the first milepost is the two-digit numeral *ab*, its numeric value can be expressed as $10a + b$. If no student used this idea, introduce it yourself. Then ask the class how to represent the other two mileposts. Students should see that the second is the two-digit numeral *ba*, which represents the number $10b + a$, and the third is the three-digit numeral *a0b*, which represents the number $100a + b$.

At this stage, you might ask, What equation can you write using this representation? Elicit the key fact in the problem—that the distances between successive mileposts in the problem are equal. This should lead students to formulate an equation like this:

$$(100a + b) - (10b + a) = (10b + a) - (10a + b)$$

If most students did not come up with this type of equation, you may want to give groups time to work with it. They should be able to simplify it to $6a = b$ and then conclude (because both *a* and *b* are single digits) that $a = 1$ and $b = 6$. The travel speed follows quickly from this.

Key Questions

How can you represent a number with specific digits in terms of powers of 10?
What equation can you write using this representation?

Story Sketches

Intent

Students sketch graphs of functions based on problem situations.

Mathematics

This activity requires students to move from a qualitative description of a situation to a sketch of a graph. The discussion afterward defines the families of linear and exponential growth functions and reviews standard equations for each.

Progression

Students sketch a graph for each of five situations. The follow-up discussion reviews and names the families of linear and exponential growth functions. The class begins a poster describing families of functions, and students create their own reference lists.

Approximate Time

25 minutes for activity (at home or in class)
35 minutes for discussion

Classroom Organization

Individuals, followed by whole-class discussion

Doing the Activity

This activity requires no introduction.

Discussing and Debriefing the Activity

Assign one of Questions 1 through 4 to each group, and give groups five minutes to prepare to present the sketch and a statement of the assumptions behind it. Because the problems are fairly open-ended and leave room for interpretation, you may want to have at least two presentations for each.

During the presentations, urge students to comment on the graphs, including corrections or improvements, and to improve their own graphs. Also discuss the appropriate choices of scales.

Questions 1 and 2: The Family of Linear Functions

The graph sketches for Questions 1 and 2 will probably be straight lines—one with positive slope, the other with negative slope. For Question 2, if students assumed the elevator's rate is not constant because the elevator goes slower as it starts and stops, only part of the graph would be straight.

Ask presenters (or the whole class) to develop at least one equation to represent each situation. **What equation can you use to represent the situation?** If needed, have them introduce a specific cost per ticket (Question 1) or a height and speed of the elevator (Question 2). It is important that students review that functions whose graphs are straight lines have a certain algebraic form.

For example, in Question 1, if a student uses P for profit, T for the number of tickets, and $10 as the price per ticket, the equation could be $P = 10T$. Some students may suggest that the graph for Question 1 should have a negative y-intercept, because of overhead expenses or an equivalent idea. If this doesn't come up, you might ask what the profit would be if no tickets were sold. This should help students focus on the idea of overhead. If they use $500 as the overhead or initial cost, they should get an equation like $P = 10T - 500$.

In Question 2, using h for height, t for time, 5 ft/s as the rate of descent, 10 feet as the height of each story, and 20 as the number of stories, the equation could be $h = 200 - 5t$.

Help students see that there are limitations in the use of a linear model for these situations. For instance, in Question 1, the value of T is limited by the theater's capacity.

For Question 2, you might ask, **What values make sense for h?** Although negative values may make sense (in terms of a basement or underground parking lot), restrictions on the range of this function do limit the value of the linear model.

If students don't bring it up, point out that the number of tickets (in Question 1) should be a whole number. Review the distinction between *continuous* and *discrete* functions by comparing the situations in Questions 1 and 2. Clarify that the situation in *Brake!* involves a continuous function even though the table provides only a discrete set of points.

Introduce the term *linear function family* to describe the set of functions whose graphs are straight lines. (*Note:* This includes constant functions, although in some contexts, mathematicians find it useful to distinguish between constant functions and nonconstant linear functions.)

Ask, **What algebraic form do linear functions have?** Students should know that a linear function is defined by an equation of the form $f(x) = a + bx$, where a and b are any two numbers. If needed, use the earlier discussion of possible equations for the ticket problem to help review this idea.

Discussion of Questions 1 and 2 is a good opportunity to point out again the several ways in which we think about functions, as it has included three of the four primary perspectives presented in this unit: situation, graph, and algebraic expression. Students will study the fourth—the table—in *Linear Tables*. They will do more work with situations involving the family of linear functions in *Back to the Basics*.

Begin "Families of Functions" Poster and Individual Reference Lists

As a class, begin the development of a poster titled "Families of Functions."

Tell students that the family of linear functions is the first of several function families they will be studying. For each family, the poster will eventually include information about each of the four aspects of functions that have been identified: an equation, a graph, a table, and a situation. Students should leave room on the poster to add new information as they learn more.

Also have students create individual records of this information for their own reference.

Questions 3 and 4: The Family of Exponential Growth Functions

Students will probably recognize Questions 3 and 4 as exponential growth problems, because interest rate problems and bacterial growth problems should be familiar to them.

Ask, What algebraic form do linear functions have? Students should come up with something of the form $f(x) = a \cdot b^x$. If they forget the coefficient a, ask about the number of bacteria at the beginning of the experiment or about the amount of money initially deposited and what the value of x is at those times.

Introduce the term *exponential growth function family* to describe the set of functions in which the y-value increases by the same fixed factor whenever x increases by a given unit amount. Have the class add this family to the poster, and give students time to make individual notes as well.

You may want to elicit other factors that might affect the growth of the bacteria colony, such as those listed here, and discuss how they might affect the graph:
- Limitations based on the size of the bacterial community
- Medical measures, such as penicillin, that might kill the colony
- Bodily defenses

Question 5

As time permits, have students share their situations and graphs for Question 5. Draw attention to which family (if either) each situation represents.

Key Questions

What equation can you use to represent the situation?
What values make sense for *h* in Question 2?
Can the number of tickets sold be a fraction?
What algebraic form do linear functions have?
What is an algebraic expression for this general type of function?

Story Sketches II

Intent

Students review the families of sine and exponential decay functions.

Mathematics

This activity is similar to *Story Sketches*, using situations involving functions in the sine and exponential decay families.

Progression

Students sketch the general shape of a graph for each of four situations and then make up a situation whose graph has the same shape as one of the given situations. The subsequent discussion defines the families of sine and exponential decay functions.

Approximate Time

30 minutes for activity (at home or in class)
20 minutes for discussion

Classroom Organization

Individuals, followed by whole-class discussion

Materials

Optional: Firm rubber ball or golf ball (to demonstrate exponential decay)

Doing the Activity

This activity requires little or no introduction.

Discussing and Debriefing the Activity

The two pairs of problems—Questions 1 and 2 and Questions 3 and 4—are similar in that in each case, the first represents a clear example of a given family while the second requires some science to understand more fully.

Question 1: The Family of Sine Functions

Have a volunteer sketch the graph asked for, and then ask, What equation describes this function, using the scales in this sketch?

Ask, What is the general form for such a function? Students should get something of the form $h(t) = a + b \sin ct$. What does each parameter, a, b, and c, represent in terms of the Ferris wheel? (The term **parameter** has been used in many IMP units, but you may want to review its meaning. It appears formally in the student book in *Families Have Many Different Members*.)

Students should recognize that a represents the height of the center of the Ferris wheel and b represents the wheel's radius. They will probably know that c is related to the rate at which the Ferris wheel turns. Clarify, if necessary, that c is the angular speed and not the period.

Introduce the term *sine function family* to describe the set of functions whose graphs repeat this up-and-down type of pattern. Try to get students to give the general form for such a function, as described previously. (The word *sinusoidal* is often used to describe functions in this family, but we will use the simpler phrase *sine function* instead.)

Tell students that the cosine function is considered a member of the sine family. To clarify this, introduce the idea of a *phase shift*, perhaps explaining it in terms of a change in the diver's starting position on the Ferris wheel. You can give students the more general form of functions in the sine family—namely,
$f(x) = a + b \sin (cx + d)$—without necessarily discussing the details of the role of d.

Ask, Are there other periodic functions besides sine functions? Clarify that functions in the sine family involve a very specific type of periodicity; that is, not every **periodic function** belongs to this family. In fact, a function can be periodic and go "up and down" without being a sine function. For example, if a person paces back and forth at a steady rate, with a fixed time at each end for turning around, the graph of the person's distance from the "center" of the pacing might look like this:

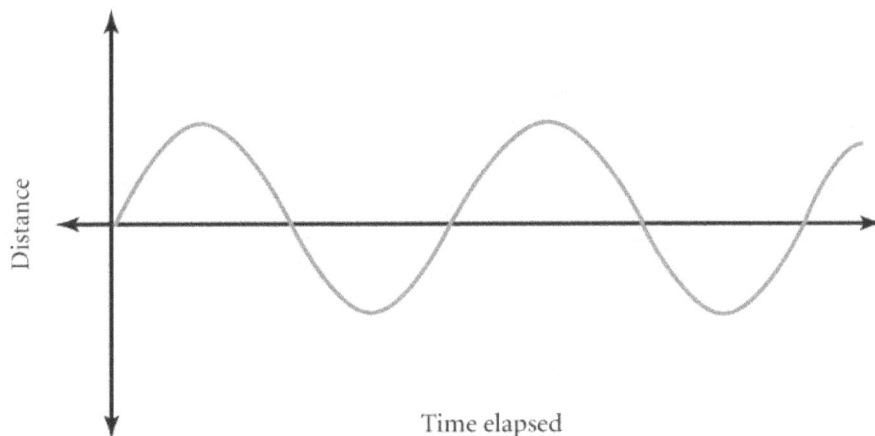

IMP Year 4, *The World of Functions* Unit, Teacher's Guide
© 2012 Interactive Mathematics Program

13

Question 2: Perhaps Like a Sine Function

For Question 2, students will probably know that the length of the day shortens and lengthens with the seasons. So, in a broad sense, the graph should have a shape similar to that of the sine function.

At least two key issues complicate the question of the appropriateness of the sine function for the situation:

- As given in the problem, the function is discrete, because the problem refers to a day-by-day measurement.
- Although the length of the day goes up and down periodically, that doesn't mean the shape is exactly that of the sine function. Determining whether it is involves the study of astronomy and is beyond the scope of this unit. You may want to suggest students research this question for extra credit.

Question 3: The Family of Exponential Decay Functions

Question 3 presents a standard example of radioactive decay. If students had trouble with this, you might suggest they pick an initial amount of carbon in the material, such as 10 kg. They should be able to get the amounts of carbon remaining for time intervals that are multiples of 20 years, but other intervals may be more difficult.

As a way of moving toward an equation, ask, for example, How much carbon will be left after 1000 years? Students will probably be able to get the answer as $10 \cdot \left(\frac{1}{2}\right)^{50}$ (because 1000 years contains fifty 20-year intervals) and then get the general expression $10 \cdot \left(\frac{1}{2}\right)^{\frac{t}{20}}$.

You can use this problem to review ideas about fractional exponents. For example, ask, How much of the carbon is lost after 10 years? Students may expect the answer to be one-fourth of the initial amount, but with discussion, they should be able to explain why this is incorrect.

Introduce the term *exponential decay function family* to describe the set of functions in which the output of the function decreases by the same fixed factor whenever the input increases by a given unit amount.

Students should see that an exponential decay function has the form $f(x) = a \cdot b^x$, which is the same as the form for an exponential growth function. Ask, How do you know whether an exponential function represents growth or decay? Students should see that for exponential decay functions, $0 < b < 1$, while for exponential growth functions, $b > 1$. You may want to ask about the case $b = 1$.

Question 4: Perhaps Like an Exponential Decay Function

Question 4 represents a more difficult situation than its predecessor. Here, too, we have a discrete function, because we are asked for the height of each bounce, rather than a graph of the ball's height over time in general. Students can only guess at the answer without a knowledge of the physics of the situation, so be prepared to accept almost any decreasing function as a reasonable guess.

Acknowledge that there is no obvious way to reason this through. Then tell students that experiments show that the ball will generally lose a certain percentage of its height with each successive bounce. You may wish to do a classroom experiment on this.

You can illustrate the numeric pattern using a specific example, such as a starting height of 30 inches and a ball that loses 40 percent of its height with each bounce. (The actual results depend on the ball and the surface.) Have students find the heights of successive bounces, which in this case would be 30 inches, 18 inches, 10.8 inches, 6.48 inches, and so on.

Then have them try to find a function for the height of the nth bounce. If they think of the initial height as the "0th" bounce, they can express the height of the nth bounce as $30 \cdot 0.6^n$ inches. You may need to discuss the idea that "losing 40 percent of the height" is the same as "multiplying the height by 0.6."

You can also use Question 4 to strengthen students' understanding of the distinction between continuous and discrete functions.

Add the families of sine and exponential decay functions to the poster, and have students add these to their individual notes as well.

Key Questions

What equation describes this function?
What is the general form for such a function?
What does each parameter represent in terms of the Ferris wheel?
Are there other periodic functions besides sine functions?
How much carbon will be left after 1000 years?
How do you know whether an exponential function represents growth or decay?

What Good Are Functions?

Intent

Students review the role of functions in understanding and solving problems.

Mathematics

Students reflect on the usefulness of functions by examining the role functions played in previous units.

Progression

Students analyze a specific function from a unit they have studied previously.

Approximate Time

30 to 35 minutes

Classroom Organization

Small groups, followed by whole-class discussion

Materials

IMP student books from Years 1 to 3
Optional: Students' portfolios for Years 1 to 3

Doing the Activity

To get students started, you might ask, *Can you can think of any examples of functions from previous units?* Also ask them to try to summarize the central problem or main idea of some previous units. Here are some units that are particularly appropriate:

- *High Dive* and *The Diver Returns*
- *Small World, Isn't It?*
- *Orchard Hideout*
- *Fireworks*
- *Cookies*
- *Is There Really a Difference?*
- *Shadows*
- *The Pit and the Pendulum*

Students may find it helpful to consult their unit portfolios, including those from Years 1 to 3, if available.

You may want to assign a specific unit to each group and have groups choose a function from that unit. If time permits, groups can also explore functions from other units.

Discussing and Debriefing the Activity

The discussion of this activity has several purposes, including these:
- Students should see a variety of familiar functions.
- Students should see various ways in which functions are useful.
- Students should look at the different ways of thinking about functions (table, graph, equation, real-world situation) and at ways to shift from one to another.

No specific content about functions needs to emerge from this discussion, so use your own judgment about how many examples to discuss. Try to include some fundamental examples, such as those mentioned below under *Orchard Hideout*, as well as more specialized examples, such as some of those used in *The Diver Returns*.

Have groups report on the functions they chose, focusing on a clear statement of the context, the quantities the function connects, and the form (graph, table, equation) in which the function was used. After each report, ask if other students have any comments. Also ask, if appropriate, in what form the function was given and how it was used.

Here are some examples of the type of descriptions students might give. These are intended only to be illustrative and to suggest questions you can ask to elicit more information and ideas.

The Diver Returns

This unit featured many functions, including these:
- The functions expressing the diver's position while he was on the Ferris wheel in terms of time elapsed. These functions were from the sine family (which includes the cosine function) and were used in terms of both algebraic expressions and graphs. They were developed from the geometry of the situation.
- The function expressing the height of the diver after he was released from the Ferris wheel in terms of time elapsed. This was a quadratic function, which was developed using some principles of physics and expressed as an algebraic equation.
- The function expressing the cart's position in terms of time. This was a linear function, which was developed based on the assumption of constant rate and expressed in terms of an algebraic equation.

In all of these cases, functions were presented primarily in the form of equations. Students combined these individual functions to develop a complex equation that told them when to let go of the diver.

Small World, Isn't It?

Students developed equations for exponential growth functions to describe a population data set and used these functions to predict when the population would be a certain size. The population information was presented initially as a table of values, but students also graphed the data set.

Orchard Hideout

Students learned about the functions for expressing area and circumference of a circle in terms of radius. They used these quadratic and linear functions to find when the radius of the trees would be large enough to provide a perfect hideout. They found the functions from the geometry of the situation and used them as equations.

Is There Really a Difference?

The χ^2 statistic itself was a function giving a measure of "rareness" in terms of the data set. (This is a function of many variables, which doesn't fit the "set of ordered pairs" definition introduced in *Brake!* If this causes confusion, you might broaden the idea of *function* using a sketch of an In-Out machine with several input hoppers. The "area of a rectangle" function is a good example.) A second function gave the probability associated with a given value of χ^2. The χ^2 function was given to students as an equation, after some plausibility discussions. The second function was given to students as a table after some simulations. (Neither of these functions fits into any of the families discussed in this unit.)

Key Question

Can you think of any examples of functions from previous units?

More Families

Intent

Students look at two more function families and are then introduced to several others.

Mathematics

This activity focuses on the families of quadratic and cubic functions. The discussion of these families is used to introduce the families of power and polynomial functions.

Progression

Students sketch graphs for two more situations, name the function families involved, and describe the general algebraic form for those families. In the subsequent discussion, they see that these problems are representative of a particular collection of function families.

Approximate Time

25 minutes for activity (at home or in class)
15 minutes for discussion

Classroom Organization

Individuals, followed by whole-class discussion

Doing the Activity

This activity requires no introduction.

Discussing and Debriefing the Activity

Begin the discussion of each problem by having a volunteer present results.

Question 1: The Family of Quadratic Functions

If the presenter for Question 1 does not bring in the general ideas from *High Dive* and *The Diver Returns*, do so yourself. Ask, What is the height at time t of an object falling freely from height h_0 and with initial velocity v_0? Help students review that the height can be given by an expression of the form $h_0 + v_0 t - 16t^2$, where h_0 and v_0 are the initial height (in feet) and velocity (in feet per second), respectively. Here, we are treating a positive value for v_0 as upward motion. Question 1 deals with a case in which v_0 is zero.

Use the term *quadratic function family* for the set of functions of the form $f(x) = ax^2 + bx + c$, where a is not zero. (*Note:* We've switched variables and rearranged the terms. Also, students already know the term *quadratic function*. Here, the focus is on the idea of these functions as a family.)

If students found an equation such as $d = 0.055s^2$ for the table in *Brake!*, point out that this is a special type of quadratic function in which two of the coefficients are zero, so these terms aren't visible.

Question 2: The Family of Cubic Functions

Students will likely express the function for Question 2 in the form $V = s^3$ and identify it as a member of the *cubic function family* (also see the next subsection, "The Family of Power Functions").

Ask students for other members of this family. If necessary, ask, What is the general form for a cubic function? Students should be able to identify this as $p(x) = ax^3 + bx^2 + cx + d$, with $a \neq 0$.

The Family of Power Functions

Students might view the volume function from Question 2 as an example of the set of functions of the form $y = x^b$. Identify these functions as members of the *power function family*. More generally, this family includes all functions of the form $y = ax^b$, where a and b are any constants (though the function is trivial if either a or b is 0). Introduce this family if students don't.

If students found an equation like $d = 0.055s^2$ for *Brake!*, identify this as another example of a **power function.**

Polynomials in General

Ask, What larger family includes linear, quadratic, and cubic equations? Students should be able to give a description such as "combinations of different powers of x with coefficients for each power." Review the term *polynomial function family* for this set of functions. Clarify that polynomials are formed by summing individual terms of the form ax^n, where n is a whole number and the coefficient a can be any real number (possibly negative or zero).

Review of Function Families

Take this opportunity to have students update the poster and their individual reference lists. The list should now include these families:

- Linear functions
- Exponential growth functions
- Exponential decay functions
- Sine functions
- Quadratic functions
- Cubic functions
- Power functions
- **Polynomial functions** (which include linear, quadratic, and cubic functions)

As needed, review the general algebraic form of functions in each family. Also discuss the general shape of a graph of a function within each family. (Students may not know the general shape for a power function or polynomial function, which is fine.)

Then ask, What other functions or families do you know? Here are some examples that might come up:
- Square-root functions and reciprocal functions (which are both part of the family of power functions, at least according to the broad definition)
- Other trigonometric functions
- **Logarithmic functions**
- Rational functions (which include reciprocal functions)
- Step functions
- Absolute value functions

Some of these families will be discussed later in the unit.

Finally ask, Can you think of situations that involve any of these types of functions? Students can add such ideas to the poster and their notes as the unit progresses.

Key Questions

What is the height at time t of an object falling freely from height h_0 and with initial velocity v_0?

What is the general form for a cubic function?

What larger family includes linear, quadratic, and cubic equations?

What other functions or families do you know?

Can you think of situations that involve any of these types of functions?

Tables

Intent

In these activities, students explore patterns in tables of several families of functions.

Mathematics

Having identified some of the major families of functions, students now learn to recognize function families from tables. They observe patterns in tables for a number of functions, such as the constant second differences for quadratic functions, and prove these patterns using the algebraic form of each function.

Progression

Linear Tables models the discovery and proof of patterns that students will undertake for other function families. Those explorations will include the tables for quadratic functions (*Quadratic Tables*, *Quadratic Tables by Algebra*, and *A General Quadratic*), exponential functions (*Exponential Tables*), cubic functions (*A Cubic Pattern*), and reciprocal functions (*Bigger Means Smaller*). Then students will turn that process around, using the patterns they have found to identify families of functions and, ultimately, specific functions from tables (*Mystery Tables* and *"Brake!" Revisited*).

Linear Tables
Story Sketches III
Quadratic Tables
Back to the Basics
Quadratic Tables by Algebra
A General Quadratic
Exponential Tables
A Cubic Pattern
POW 3: A Spin on Transitivity
Mystery Tables
"Brake!" Revisited
Bigger Means Smaller

Linear Tables

Intent

Students look for patterns in the tables of linear functions.

Mathematics

Linear Tables is the first of a sequence of activities in which students investigate tables of values for different families of functions. In this activity, students will gain further insight into principles they already know about tables for linear functions. In particular, they will see how patterns in such tables relate to the algebraic form of the function.

Progression

Working in groups, students look for patterns in the tables of various linear functions, using equally spaced inputs. The teacher leads the class in periodic discussion as groups move on to prove their results algebraically. Finally, students explain why their patterns make sense in terms of the graphs of linear functions and in terms of the situations from which the functions arise.

Approximate Time

35 minutes

Classroom Organization

Small groups, interspersed with whole-class discussion

Doing the Activity

Linear Tables is perhaps best done as a blend of group work and whole-class discussion, with groups working for short periods and then sharing ideas in a teacher-led discussion. For that reason, we are including detailed discussion ideas here rather than in a separate "discussion" section. In subsequent activities, students will do similar work for other families of functions.

Working on Questions 1 and 2

Begin by having groups work on Questions 1 and 2. Be sure they understand that "equally spaced inputs" means the entries in the *In* column increase by the same amount from one row to the next. If their calculators have a table feature, encourage students to use it.

Students probably already know (perhaps with different depths of understanding) that with equally spaced inputs, the outputs for a linear function will also increase (or decrease) by the same amount. Therefore, this idea should come out fairly quickly as groups start to explore.

It is important that students see, through examples, that this works for *any* linear function and for *any* equal spacing of inputs. If groups seem clear about increases of 1 from one row to the next, urge them to vary the increase.

Discussion of Questions 1 and 2

Bring the class together to discuss what groups have discovered, beginning with the specific example of Question 1—the function defined by the equation $f(x) = 4x + 7$. Students should see that the difference in successive *Out* values is 4 times the difference in successive *In* values. Be sure to include examples in which the increase is different from 1.

Then have students share what they have seen about tables of other linear functions. Focus on specific examples, as this may help them to state the general principle more clearly.

Then ask, How can you state what you have discovered as a general principle? They might formulate the property like this:

> **If *f* is any linear function and we make an In-Out table for *f* using equally spaced inputs, the table will also have equally spaced outputs.**

Working on Question 3

For clarity, have students try to express the task in their own words. They are to prove that any function *f* of the form $f(x) = ax + b$ has a table with the property just described and that this is the case no matter what "equal spacing" is used.

If groups have trouble getting started, suggest they begin with a specific example (such as that in Question 1) and prove that for this function, the property holds for any equally spaced set of inputs.

You can use the sequence of questions that follows to lead a discussion to arrive at the proof. At any point in this development, either ask groups to try to complete the process or continue with a whole-class discussion. (*Note:* Part of the purpose of this discussion is to create a model for students' work on subsequent activities for other families of functions. Thus, although the conclusion about tables for linear functions may be "obvious," and students may think a proof is unnecessary, they are doing a useful type of reasoning.)

You might begin by returning to the specific examples discussed earlier. Ask, How might you prove for a specific function that any equally spaced inputs give equally spaced outputs? The word "any" should be a good hint that students are looking for variables.

Here, we use the specific example from Question 1, $f(x) = 4x + 7$, starting with a variable for the initial input and an interval of 1 between inputs.

For instance, suppose students call the initial input w. They should be able to fill in a table something like this (although they may immediately simplify the last two outputs to $4w + 11$ and $4w + 15$):

In	Out
w	$4w + 7$
$w + 1$	$4(w + 1) + 7$
$w + 2$	$4(w + 2) + 7$

Ask students what they should do next. If they understand what the task is, they will see they need to show that the increase in the output from one row of the table to the next is constant. That is, they should find the difference between the first two outputs and the difference between the second and third outputs, and show they are the same. Thus, they should find these two differences:

$$[4(w + 1) + 7] - [4w + 7]$$
$$[4(w + 2) + 7] - [4(w + 1) + 7]$$

and see they are both equal to 4.

At this point, you might either do the same sort of analysis for the general linear function or work with the specific function using a variable to represent the equal spacing. Here, we follow the first path and then generalize to arbitrary spacing.

Using the equation $y = ax + b$ for the function, the table might look like this:

In	Out
w	$aw + b$
$w + 1$	$a(w + 1) + b$
$w + 2$	$a(w + 2) + b$

As in the specific example, students should work out the two differences from one row to the next:

$$[a(w + 1) + b] - [aw + b]$$
$$[a(w + 2) + b] - [a(w + 1) + b]$$

Students will need to pay careful attention to brackets, parentheses, and signs as they work out these differences.

Elicit the idea that the common difference, a, is consistent with the numeric value of 4 they found for the specific function $y = 4x + 7$.

A Further Generalization

If students generalized further or are interested in pursuing this, have them look at the case of the general interval between inputs for a general linear function. (You may need to take the lead in setting up this analysis, but students will probably follow the reasoning fairly well.) This generalization involves a table like this one:

In	Out
w	$aw + b$
$w + c$	$a(w + c) + b$
$w + 2c$	$a(w + 2c) + b$

Students will need to expand the output expressions to find the differences. For instance, help them see that the difference between the first and second outputs here is

$$[a(w + c) + b] - [aw + b]$$

and that this can be expanded to

$$[aw + ac + b] - [aw + b]$$

which is equal to ac.

Once again, the difference between successive outputs is the same in each case: ac.

Mention that this sort of analysis constitutes a *proof* of what students have long seen in numeric examples. It may also be worth noting that the algebra of the proof in this case is fairly simple, but can serve as a model of how to proceed with more complex families of functions.

Questions 4 and 5

In addition to having students provide a satisfactory algebraic explanation of the numeric pattern for In-Out tables of linear functions, it's helpful to have them connect this pattern to both the graphical and (as time permits) situational perspectives of linear functions.

In terms of graphs (Question 4), students should be able to connect this property of In-Out tables to the concept of slope. That is, they should see that the fact that "equal 'overs' produce equal 'ups'" means that graphs of linear functions are straight lines, with constant slopes (or "rates of change"). They might even refer to the concept of similar triangles.

Bring out that a, the x-coefficient in our notation, represents the slope and that the "equal spacing" in the inputs for the table is the same as the "over." Ask students to connect that observation with their proof that the difference in successive outputs is ac. They should be able to reason that the "up" (the difference in outputs) should be the product of the slope (a) and the "over" (c).

Question 5 is included for groups who finish early. If necessary, suggest students think about Question 1 from *Story Sketches*, in which each additional ticket increases the profit by the same amount. To deal with different intervals for the change in inputs, they could consider the increase in profit for each group of five tickets, for example.

Key Questions

How can you state what you have discovered as a general principle?
How might you prove for a specific function that any equally spaced inputs give equally spaced outputs?

Story Sketches III

Intent

Students sketch graphs or make tables for more functions based on real-world situations.

Mathematics

This activity is similar to *Story Sketches* and *Story Sketches II*. The situation in the first question produces a hyperbola, and the discussion might be expanded into developing an equation for the situation and showing that the graph of that equation is indeed a hyperbola.

Progression

Students sketch graphs or make tables for several real-world situations.

Approximate Time

20 minutes for activity (at home or in class)
10 minutes for discussion

Classroom Organization

Individuals, followed by whole-class discussion

Doing the Activity

This activity needs no introduction.

Discussing and Debriefing the Activity

Have one or two students share their results on each problem.

If the first student presenting Question 1 does not use a diagram of the situation, try to elicit one. The situation might be represented as shown here:

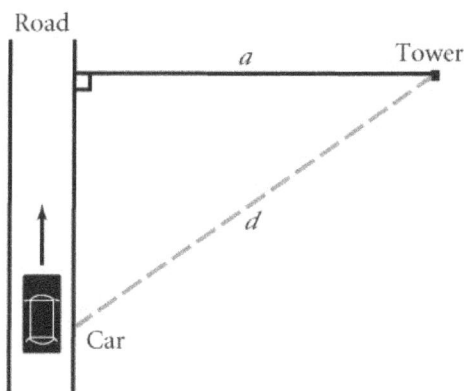

The distance *a* is fixed, and the distance *d* varies as a function of time. Thus, the graph should show the distance *d* decreasing as the car reaches the point due west of the tower and then increasing as the car continues north. If the student assumed (consciously or not) speed was constant, the graph should be symmetric about the time when the car is due west of the tower.

The supplemental activity *A Hyperbolic Approach* asks students to get an explicit equation for *d* in terms of *t* under the assumption of constant speed and then to show that the graph of that equation is a hyperbola. (Because the second question of that activity involves concepts from later in this unit, it is best to assign this supplemental activity later.)

For Question 2, if students only consider the time until the pie is done, the graph or table should show temperature gradually rising toward 325° (starting from room temperature) and then leveling off (with perhaps some slight oscillation during a mostly level period). If the graph or table also includes the period after the oven is turned off, it should show the temperature going down after the earlier level period and then leveling off again at room temperature.

For Question 3, if students do not consider daylight savings time, the graph will probably look something like a sine curve (with a "low"—earliest rising sun—in June, and a "high"—latest rising sun—in December). If daylight savings time is considered, then for the section of the graph showing that period (roughly, mid March through early November), the times for sunrise would all be increased by one hour.

The graphs in Questions 1 and 2 are both continuous. The graph in Question 3 is discrete, but because it includes many points, it may appear to be continuous, and students may wish to think of it that way.

Quadratic Tables

Intent

Students explore patterns in tables of quadratic functions.

Mathematics

As students find and describe patterns in the tables of quadratic functions, they will discover that the second difference for any particular function appears to be constant.

Progression

Working in groups, students look for patterns in the tables of several quadratic functions, using a variety of equally spaced inputs. They also examine how the pattern varies from one quadratic function to another. The follow-up discussion focuses on the second difference.

Approximate Time

40 minutes

Classroom Organization

Small groups, followed by whole-class discussion

Doing the Activity

As groups work, you may need to urge them to examine more examples within the family and to record their observations clearly. The emphasis here is on the search for patterns. Later activities will focus on algebraic proof of the patterns students find in this activity.

Based on their experience with *Linear Tables*, students will likely begin by looking at the difference between successive terms in the *Out* column. If they are having difficulty finding a pattern, you might explicitly ask them to examine these differences. **What did you look at in *Linear Tables* to find a pattern? Will that help you here?** They will probably see that the differences increase (or decrease) by a fixed amount from one row to the next; that is, the second differences are constant. (The term *second difference* will be introduced in the discussion of this activity, although you might use it with individual groups as well.) Some students may already know, or may discover quite quickly, that quadratic functions have constant second differences. Urge them to learn more, as described in the next subsection.

Exploring the Details of Second Differences

Once groups see that second differences are constant, urge them to look for more details, so they can generalize their results for Question 3. If they have focused only on input differences of 1, have them vary the input difference. If they have considered only quadratics in which the coefficient of x^2 is 1, have them consider other possibilities. Suggest specifically that they examine what determines the numeric value of the second difference, perhaps pointing out that the difference for linear functions depends on the coefficient of x (and on the difference in the *In* terms).

Discussing and Debriefing the Activity

Questions 1 and 2

Begin with a few presentations of specific examples that groups examined in Questions 1 and 2, eliciting as much variety as possible. Presenters should observe that for quadratic functions, the difference in outputs from row to row of the table is not constant. Instead, the differences themselves are increasing by a fixed amount.

Introduce the term *second difference* for "the difference between the differences." You can use a multicolumn table like this one to help students understand this term. This example uses the quadratic function defined by the equation $f(x) = x^2 + 3x - 2$.

In (x)	Out ($x^2 + 3x - 2$)	Difference in outputs	Second difference
3	16		
		10	
4	26		2
		12	
5	38		2
		14	
6	52		2
		16	
7	68		

Help students describe the pattern they saw using the term *second difference*. For example, they might state it like this:

> **Any In-Out table for a quadratic function using equally spaced inputs will have constant second differences.**

Explain that for now, at least, this statement is still merely a conjecture. Some students may see the pattern but have a hard time stating it clearly, especially while they are still becoming familiar with the terminology. Some may have seen this pattern in the data set in the activity *Brake!* They will return to that situation in *"Brake!" Revisited* and *Better Braking*.

If students have not yet done so, have them verify this statement for specific cases with input differences other than 1 and coefficients of x^2 other than 1.

Question 3

Some groups may have seen patterns in how the second difference depends on the spacing of the inputs and on the coefficient of x^2. If they are not ready for this level of detail, you can delay this issue; it will be part of the discussion of *A General Quadratic*.

A Pattern Is Not a Proof

Be sure students realize that although they have seen the pattern of constant second differences in many examples, they have not proved that this pattern applies to every quadratic function. Remind them that they did prove the corresponding pattern for linear functions, and tell them that they will prove the pattern for quadratic functions, too (at least for the case in which the difference in inputs is 1).

Key Question

What did you look at in *Linear Tables* to find a pattern? Will that help you here?

Back to the Basics

Intent

Students see the set of linear functions as a two-parameter family.

Mathematics

This activity continues students' work with linear functions and reviews how to fit a linear function to information in a situation. The discussion will also address the connection between the algebra and the graph of a linear function.

Progression

Students solve four problem situations using the assumption of linearity. A final question asks them to consider whether the linear model was appropriate in each case. The subsequent discussion looks at each problem in terms of graphs, tables, and equations.

Approximate Time

25 to 30 minutes for activity (at home or in class)
15 to 20 minutes for discussion

Classroom Organization

Individuals, followed by whole-class discussion

Doing the Activity

This activity requires no introduction.

Discussing and Debriefing the Activity

The discussion should emphasize the connection between the algebra and the geometry, bringing out that a linear function of the form $f(x) = ax + b$ has two parameters and that a line is determined by two points.

Question 1

Begin the discussion by having a student present Question 1, which will probably seem trivial. If the presenter does not use a table, ask, What would a table for this function look like? You may want to get the student to articulate that the cost of n calculators is n times the cost of one calculator.

Have a volunteer give an explicit algebraic equation describing the problem (for instance, $C = 12.95n$, where n is the number of calculators and C is the cost). You might hold off discussing the graph or table until the comparison of Questions 1 and 2.

Question 2, and Comparison with Question 1

One approach to Question 2 is to play devil's advocate, suggesting that if the hiker reaches 3000 feet at 3 p.m., he will reach 6000 feet by 6 p.m. Act as if this is exactly analogous to Question 1, with the hiker's altitude being 1000 feet times the hour on the clock. Emphasize that this is reasonable because the hiker is climbing at a steady rate. That is, the hiker's altitude goes up the same amount each hour, just as the cost of calculators goes up the same amount for each additional calculator.

Students will probably recognize that this proportional reasoning is not valid. Be sure to have them explain why: **Why does this reasoning work in Question 1 and not in Question 2?**

If needed, ask them to consider the information given in the two problems. **What information does each problem provide about the graph (or table)?** Each appears to give just one point of the graph (or one row of an In-Out table). Question 1 says, in effect, that the graph goes through the point (30, 388.50), while Question 2 says that it goes through (3, 3000).

Ask, **How is the information different in the two problems?** Bring out that Question 1 includes the implicit assumption that it costs $0 to buy 0 calculators— that is, that the graph goes through the point (0, 0).

You might ask, **What assumption about the hiker would be analogous to the assumption about calculators in Question 1?** For instance, students might say he was at sea level (an altitude of 0 feet) at noon (which is like "0 p.m.").

Question 3

Question 3 is a good example to look at from different perspectives.
* Using a table: Successive rows increase the number of miles by 50 and the cost by $4.
* Using an equation: The cost for n miles is found to be $25 + 0.08n$ dollars.
* Using a graph: The points (200, 41) and (250, 45) are plotted, and we look for the y-coordinate of the point where $x = 50$.

You might also ask, **How can you tell that the problem is solvable without actually solving it?** The geometry provides a way to explain this. That is, students may be able to articulate that two points are given, so there is a unique line that goes through them, and they simply have to find out where this line has a y-value (cost) of $50.

Question 4

Students need to make some assumptions to solve Question 4. For instance, has Chloe already spent her Day 6 money when we find her on the beach? Does she spend the full $75 on Day 10, when she leaves? The problem is easily amenable to the use of both a table and an algebraic expression (such as $784 - 75n$, with $n = 0$ representing Day 6), and you can probably deal with these approaches quickly.

Focus the discussion on this question: How is the information provided in this problem reflected in the graph? In Questions 1 and 3, students were essentially given two points for each graph. Elicit the idea that in Question 4, they have the slope and a single point, rather than two points.

Use this example to help students articulate the principle that a line can also be determined by a point and a slope. It may help to remind them that knowing both a point and a slope will allow them to obtain a second point. They can then use the idea that two points determine a line.

Linear Functions Are a Two-Parameter Family

This problem provides a good opportunity to focus on the two-parameter nature of linear functions. Bring out that "knowing" a linear function requires two pieces of information, which can be any of these combinations:
- Two points
- One point and the slope
- The coefficients a and b in the expression $ax + b$

Because "knowing" a linear function requires two pieces of information, we describe the family of linear functions as a *two-parameter family*.

Not Everything Is Linear

Before beginning the discussion of Question 5, raise the idea that simply having two points for a graph does not automatically tell what the graph is, because not every situation is linear. One way to bring this point out is to ask, Is knowing two points of a graph (or two rows of an In-Out table) always enough information to tell you what the function is?

For instance, you might ask what function is represented by this In-Out table:

In	Out
1	3
2	5

The linear equation $y = 2x + 1$ fits this table, but the nonlinear equations $y = x^2 - x + 3$ and $y = 2^x + 1$ do as well.

Question 5

Questions 5a and 5b concern whether a linear model is appropriate for each of Questions 1 to 4. There are two distinct issues here.

For Question 5a, which asks whether the problem is linear as written, have students identify phrases or elements that suggest linearity. **What clues in the problem tell you that it's supposed to be linear?** For example, they might mention "climbing steadily" in Question 2 or "per-mile charge" in Question 3.

For Question 5b, have students offer pros and cons for treating the situations as linear. Here are some possible considerations:
- Question 1: The situation sounds linear until one thinks of discounts for large quantities. Also, the cost of calculators would consist of discrete points with whole-number independent values rather than a continuous line.
- Question 2: Hikers do not usually climb at a steady pace. They might grow tired, and the steepness of the trail might vary.
- Question 3: Rental rates such as those described here are quite common, but other factors might be included in the rate.
- Question 4: Although Chloe is described as spending "$75 a day," it would be unusual for a person to spend money at a constant daily rate during a vacation.

Key Questions

Why does this reasoning work in Question 1 and not in Question 2?
What information does each problem provide about the graph (or table)?
How is the information different in the two problems?
What assumption about the hiker would be analogous to the assumption about calculators in Question 1?
How can you tell that the problem is solvable without actually solving it?
How is the information provided in this problem reflected in the graph?
Is knowing two points of a graph (or two rows of an In-Out table) always enough information to tell you what the function is?
What clues in the problem tell you that it's supposed to be linear?

Quadratic Tables by Algebra

Intent

Students develop a partial proof of the pattern they found in tables of quadratic functions.

Mathematics

In this activity, students prove algebraically, for a specific quadratic function, the pattern of constant second differences that they saw in *Quadratic Tables*. This proof is limited to the case in which the difference in inputs is equal to 1. In *A General Quadratic*, they will generalize this proof to the case of an arbitrary quadratic function.

Progression

Students complete a table for a given quadratic function and then find the first and second differences. They repeat this action, substituting w for the initial input, compare their results to those from the first table, and explain why this constitutes a proof that the given function has constant second differences.

Students will need their results from this activity for *A General Quadratic*.

Approximate Time

35 minutes

Classroom Organization

Individuals, followed by whole-class discussion

Doing the Activity

If students need help getting started on Question 2, bring out that $f(w)$ is found simply by replacing x with w in the equation $f(x) = x^2 + 2x + 3$. Similarly, students should find $f(w + 1)$ by replacing x with $w + 1$.

To answer Question 2b, they will need to expand expressions like $(w + 1)^2 + 2(w + 1) + 3$ and find differences between such expressions.

You might have each group prepare a presentation of a different part of this activity.

Discussing and Debriefing the Activity

Information for Questions 1 and 2 is summarized in the tables below. To find the differences in the outputs for the second table, students will need to expand the *Out* expressions and perform the subtraction.

In	Out	Difference in outputs	Second difference
7	66		
		17	
8	83		2
		19	
9	102		2
		21	
10	123		2

In	Out	Difference in outputs	Second difference
w	$w^2 + 2w + 3$		
		$2w + 3$	
$w + 1$	$(w + 1)^2 + 2(w + 1) + 3$		2
		$2w + 5$	
$w + 2$	$(w + 2)^2 + 2(w + 2) + 3$		2
		$2w + 7$	
$w + 3$	$(w + 3)^2 + 2(w + 3) + 3$		2

Ask, How are these two tables related? For instance, replacing w by 7 in the expression $2w + 3$ (in the "Difference in outputs" column) gives the corresponding value of 17 from the previous table.

Have students explain why the second table *proves* (for this particular quadratic function) that the second difference is equal to 2 whenever the difference between inputs is equal to 1.

Key Question

How are these two tables related?

A General Quadratic

Intent

Students complete the proof that second differences in quadratic tables are constant, using the algebraic form of the functions.

Mathematics

This activity generalizes the work of *Quadratic Tables by Algebra*, extending the proof that second differences for a specific quadratic function are constant to the case of a general quadratic function.

Progression

Students examine the first and second differences in a table for the general quadratic function, $g(x) = ax^2 + bx + c$, first using numeric inputs and then using w as the initial input. The subsequent discussion optionally takes the proof one step further, using h rather than 1 as the interval between inputs.

Approximate Time

25 to 30 minutes for activity (at home or in class)
15 to 20 minutes for discussion

Classroom Organization

Individuals, followed by whole-class discussion

Doing the Activity

This activity requires no introduction.

Discussing and Debriefing the Activity

Questions 1 and 2

The tables below show the information for Questions 1 and 2. An important element of the discussion should be the recognition that the second table constitutes a proof. Specifically, the table proves that for the case in which the inputs are increasing by 1, second differences are constant for any quadratic function. Because the second difference, $2a$, does not involve w, this means the second difference will be the same for any sequence of inputs that differ by 1.

In	Out	Difference in outputs	Second difference
7	$49a + 7b + c$		
		$15a + b$	
8	$64a + 8b + c$		$2a$
		$17a + b$	
9	$81a + 9b + c$		$2a$
		$19a + b$	
10	$100a + 10b + c$		

In	Out	Difference in outputs	Second difference
w	$aw^2 + bw + c$		
		$2aw + a + b$	
$w + 1$	$a(w + 1)^2 + b(w + 1) + c$		$2a$
		$2aw + 3a + b$	
$w + 2$	$a(w + 2)^2 + b(w + 2) + c$		$2a$
		$2aw + 5a + b$	
$w + 3$	$a(w + 3)^2 + b(w + 3) + c$		

As with the discussion of *Linear Tables*, the general analysis not only proves that second differences are constant, but also gives an algebraic expression for the second difference (for the case in which inputs differ by 1). Students can see that the second difference depends only on the coefficient of x^2 in the function. This is an observation they might not have made simply from examining specific examples.

You might have students verify that the second difference is equal to $2a$ using a specific example with $a \neq 1$.

Question 3

You might refer to the second part of the previous table, which uses both a general quadratic function and a general initial input, to confirm examples that were specific in some respect. For instance, replacing w with 7 in the expression $2aw + a + b$ (in the "Difference in outputs" column) can be used to confirm the expression $15a + b$ (in the first table)

Similarly, replacing a with 1 and b with 2 in the expression $2aw + a + b$ (leaving w as a variable) confirms the expression $2w + 3$ in the table for Question 2a of *Quadratic Tables by Algebra*. And the general second difference of $2a$ confirms the specific second difference of 2 in both tables in that activity.

Optional: Arbitrary Equal Spacing for Inputs

The further generalization discussed here may be difficult for students, so use your judgment about whether to pursue it.

Ask students to look at what happens when the increase in the input is represented by a variable. Representing this increase by h produces this table, which generalizes several rows of the table from Question 2:

In	Out	Difference in outputs	Second difference
w	$aw^2 + bw + c$		
		$2awh + ah^2 + bh$	
$w + h$	$a(w + h)^2 + b(w + h) + c$		$2ah^2$
		$2awh + 3ah^2 + bh$	
$w + 2h$	$a(w + 2h)^2 + b(w + 2h) + c$		

Again, the second difference does not involve w, so this constitutes a proof that second differences are constant for any quadratic function as long as the inputs are equally spaced. Students can verify that replacing h with 1 gives the same values as in the previous table.

This table also yields the expression $2ah^2$ for the second difference in terms of a and h. If students are given an In-Out table that shows constant second differences, this expression can be used to find the value of a.

Another approach to thinking about the pattern is to see that for a given quadratic function and fixed choice of h, the differences themselves form a linear expression in w. A general algebraic analysis shows that differences for a polynomial function are one degree lower than the polynomial itself. If we think of a constant as a polynomial of degree zero, it follows that the second differences of a quadratic are constant.

The Converse of Constant Second Differences

Students have just seen that if a function is quadratic, its table has constant second differences (when the inputs are equally spaced). It turns out that the converse is also true; that is, if a function has a table with constant second differences, it must be quadratic. This idea is explored in the supplemental activity *From Second Differences to Quadratics*.

In *"Brake!" Revisited*, students can use this converse to conclude that they should look for a quadratic function to fit the table. Although they may not have proved the converse, it is nevertheless quite reasonable to guess that a quadratic function is a likely candidate for a function to fit that table.

Supplemental Activity

From Second Differences to Quadratics (extension) asks students to develop a partial proof that if a function has constant second differences, it is a quadratic function.

Exponential Tables

Intent

Students find and describe patterns in the tables of exponential functions.

Mathematics

Students will find two patterns in the tables of exponential functions in this activity: the ratio of consecutive outputs is constant, and the ratio of differences of consecutive pairs of outputs is constant. They will and try to prove these patterns using the algebraic form of the functions.

Progression

This activity is very similar to *Linear Tables* and *Quadratic Tables*. As before, the emphasis is on finding and proving patterns. Working in groups, students look for patterns in the tables of exponential functions by dividing consecutive outputs, give a general proof of their results, and then look for another pattern by subtracting consecutive outputs.

Approximate Time

50 to 65 minutes

Classroom Organization

Small groups, followed by whole-class discussion

Doing the Activity

Before groups begin, ask the class, What is the general algebraic form of exponential functions? Students may recall that the general form is $k \cdot b^{cx}$. Suggest they begin their work with the less general expression b^x. When groups have worked through Questions 1 and 2 with this special case, they can go back and deal with more general examples, perhaps next treating exponential functions of the form b^{cx} and then going on to the most general form as time allows.

Question 3 can be assigned as more advanced work for groups that complete Questions 1 and 2.

The suggestions here are based on the assumption that students will create an In-Out table in which the inputs increase by 1 from row to row. More ambitious groups can look at the general case of equally spaced inputs.

For Question 1, groups should see that the ratio of consecutive terms is constant. This is similar to the pattern for linear functions, where the *difference* of consecutive terms is constant.

To prove this pattern, students will need to simplify expressions like $\dfrac{b^{x+1}}{b^x}$. You may want to use this occasion to review the additive law of exponents. If necessary, suggest students look at numeric examples, such as $\dfrac{3^7}{3^6}$. They should simplify them in this form, rather than finding the numeric values of the numerator and denominator separately.

For Question 3, groups will likely see the pattern that the differences themselves form an In-Out table for an exponential function. If any groups finish early, you might suggest they try to prove this, using the form of the function.

As groups complete parts of the problem, ask them to prepare presentations. Begin presentations when groups seem to have gone as far as they can.

Discussing and Debriefing the Activity

For Question 1, the pattern for the table of an exponential function is similar to that for a linear function, except that it involves multiplication instead of addition. One way of expressing the pattern is to say that each output is a certain fixed number times the previous output.

If students expressed this in other ways, encourage this characterization. They should check for this pattern in their own tables.

This is a good opportunity to have students work with more general examples than they may have used previously. For instance, if they worked with input differences equal to 1, you might have them work with other equally spaced inputs.

For example, using the function $f(x) = 3 \cdot 2^x$, they might make this In-Out table, using an initial x-value of 5 and a fixed difference of 0.3:

In	Out
5	96
5.3	118.2
5.6	145.5
5.9	179.1

The three ratios $\frac{179.1}{145.5}$, $\frac{145.5}{118.2}$, and $\frac{118.2}{96}$ are all equal (at least to within round-off error).

For the proof in Question 2, using the function given by the equation $f(x) = 3 \cdot 2^x$, students might use this table:

In	Out
w	$3 \cdot 2^w$
$w + 1$	$3 \cdot 2^{w+1}$

They should see that the second output is 2 times the previous one. That is,

$$\frac{3 \cdot 2^{w+1}}{3 \cdot 2^w} = \frac{2 \cdot 2^w}{2^w} = 2$$

Because the ratio of successive terms does not involve w, it will be the same for any two rows of the table.

The Completely General Case

Building on their experience with previous activities, you might encourage groups to look at the most general case. That is, they can use the exponential function defined by the equation $y = k \cdot b^{cx}$, use w as an initial input, and use h to represent the difference between successive inputs. This leads to a table like this:

In	Out
w	$k \cdot b^{cw}$
$w + h$	$k \cdot b^{c(w+h)}$

Groups should be able to simplify the ratio

$$\frac{k \cdot b^{c(w+h)}}{k \cdot b^{cw}}$$

to b^{ch}. As with the simpler case, this ratio does not involve w, so it will be the same for all pairs of successive outputs that have a difference of h for the inputs.

Question 3

For Question 3, if students are looking at a function of the form $f(x) = k \cdot b^x$, with a difference of 1 between successive inputs, they may see that the differences between consecutive outputs represent an exponential function. For example, using the function $f(x) = 4 \cdot 3^x$ and a starting input of 2, they would get this table:

In	Out	Differences
2	36	
		72
3	108	
		216
4	324	
		648
5	972	

Here, each difference is 3 times the preceding difference.

If any students attempt to prove this pattern for input differences of 1, they might use this sequence of equations:

$$k \cdot b^{x + 1} - k \cdot b^x = k \cdot b^x \cdot b - k \cdot b^x$$
$$= k \cdot b^x (b - 1)$$
$$= k(b - 1) \cdot b^x$$

For the table, we have $k = 4$ and $b = 3$. For instance, with $x = 2$, the difference is $4 \cdot (3 - 1) \cdot 3^2$, which gives the value 72 in the table. The proof for more general exponential functions and differences in inputs is similar.

Key Question

What is the general algebraic form of exponential functions?

A Cubic Pattern

Intent

Students find and prove patterns in the tables of cubic functions.

Mathematics

This activity takes the algebraic analysis of the last several days to another level. The analysis for cubic functions is very similar to the work with quadratic functions. Whereas second differences are constant in the tables of quadratic functions, students will find that third differences are constant in the tables of cubic functions.

Progression

Students make a table for the simplest of cubic functions, find a pattern in the table, and use algebra to prove that pattern for the case in which inputs differ by 1. The subsequent discussion can be very brief, since the work is very similar to that in *Quadratic Tables*.

Approximate Time

30 minutes for activity (at home or in class)
10 to 15 minutes for discussion

Classroom Organization

Individuals, followed by whole-class discussion

Doing the Activity

This activity requires no introduction.

Discussing and Debriefing the Activity

Students are likely to see that in the case of a cubic function, it is the *third* differences that are constant. The table below, for the function $f(x) = x^3$, illustrates this.

In	Out	Differences in outputs	Second difference	Third difference
1	1			
		7		
2	8		12	
		19		6
3	27		18	
		37		6
4	64		24	
		61		6
5	125		30	
		91		
6	216			

If students were unable to work through the algebraic details of why third differences are constant for this cubic function, you may want to conduct the analysis as a class. The next table gives details, showing that when inputs differ by 1, the third difference is equal to 6 no matter what the initial input is.

In	Out	Difference in outputs	Second difference	Third difference
w	w^3			
		$3w^2 + 3w + 1$		
$w + 1$	$(w + 1)^3 =$ $w^3 + 3w^2 + 3w + 1$		$6w + 6$	
		$3w^2 + 9w + 7$		6
$w + 2$	$(w + 2)^3 =$ $w^3 + 6w^2 + 12w + 8$		$6w + 12$	
		$3w^2 + 15w + 19$		
$w + 3$	$(w + 3)^3 =$ $w^3 + 9w^2 + 27w + 27$			

You might have students connect this general table to the specific one that precedes it. For instance, have them substitute 3 for w in the expression $3w^2 + 3w + 1$, the first item under "Difference in outputs." They should get 37 and see that this corresponds to the value 37 in the preceding table that represents the difference between inputs of 3 and 4.

You may also want to point out that the first difference is a quadratic expression in terms of the initial input. Thus, when the input increases from $x = w$ to $x = w + 1$, the output increases by $3w^2 + 3w + 1$. Similarly, the increase from $x = w + 1$ to $x = w + 2$ is $3(w + 1)^2 + 3(w + 1) + 1$, and so on. Because the difference column is a quadratic function, *its* second differences, which are the third differences of the original function, are constant.

Use your judgment about how much time, if any, to spend on generalizations of this pattern. It is true that third differences are constant for any cubic function (with any fixed amount for the increase in inputs), but the algebra of proving this is not very exciting.

You might ask students to make a conjecture about the table for a polynomial of degree 4. If they make the natural conjecture—that fourth differences are constant—you can either leave this for them to prove or simply confirm that this conjecture is correct.

POW 3: A Spin on Transitivity

Intent

Students explore transitivity in a probability context.

Mathematics

Relationships are said to be *transitive* when we can reason in a manner such as "*A > B,* and *B > C,* so *A > C.*" This POW explores some nontransitive relationships.

This problem involves both reasoning and guess-and-check. In addition, students will probably need to devise a coding and record-keeping system to be successful.

Progression

This POW presents students with a set of three spinners and a simple game where each player spins his or her spinner a single time and the players compare their results. Part I asks students to calculate the probabilities associated with all the two-player matches that are possible in order to decide which spinner is best in each case. The POW then points out that in a three-player game, the spinners are nontransitive. Part II asks students to explore a number of situations involving transitivity in spinners.

Approximate Time

10 minutes for introduction
2 to 4 hours for activity (at home)
15 minutes for whole-class presentations and discussion

Classroom Organization

Individuals, followed by whole-class presentations and discussion

Doing the Activity

You may want to point out explicitly that the write-up for this POW does not follow the usual format.

On the day before the POW is due, select three students to make presentations on the following day.

Discussing and Debriefing the Activity

Have the three students begin with presentations on Part I, and go over any questions students have about the specific results.

For Part II, have the presenters describe their results, and have other students contribute additional ideas they discovered or other questions they investigated. If there are any questions in Part II that no one solved, you might just leave them as open questions.

The answer to the first question posed in Part II is yes; it is possible to create another set of spinners as described.

For the second question, the answer is no. One explanation for why there is no such system of spinners is that the spinner with 1 on it can never be better than any other spinner. It would lose whenever 1 came up, giving it a probability of winning of no more than 0.5.

For the third question, the answer is yes. In fact, there is more than one set of spinners fitting the given conditions.

Mystery Tables

Intent

Students find functions to fit specific tables.

Mathematics

In this activity, students put together what they have learned about tables in the last few days. They are not expected to have memorized the details of the patterns, but they should know that first differences in linear tables are constant, that second differences in quadratic tables are constant, and that ratios in exponential tables are constant.

Progression

Presented with tables for six functions, students decide to which family each function belongs and find an algebraic expression for each one.

Approximate Time

30 to 40 minutes for activity (at home or in class)
10 to 15 minutes for discussion

Classroom Organization

Individuals, followed by whole-class discussion

Doing the Activity

This activity requires little or no introduction.

Discussing and Debriefing the Activity

Ask for volunteers to provide equations for each of the six functions and to explain how they found their answers. How did you get the equation? Specifically, elicit explanations of how they decided on the family each function belongs to.

There may be a variety of approaches, so ask other students to share alternative strategies. Did anyone use another strategy? If there are any problems that no one gets, you might leave them open and offer extra credit for the answers.

Here are possible equations for the functions:

- $f(x) = x^2 + 1$
- $g(x) = x^2 - 2x$
- $h(x) = -5x + 2$
- $F(x) = 0.5 \cdot 2^x$ (or 2^{x-1})
- $G(x) = 2x^3 - 4x$
- $H(x) = 3 \cdot 0.5^x$

Key Questions

How did you get the equation?
Did anyone use another strategy?

"Brake!" Revisited

Intent

Students apply their new knowledge to the opening problem of the unit.

Mathematics

Students look back at the data table they worked with in *Brake!* and analyze it in terms of the patterns they have observed for various families of functions.

Progression

Students revisit the table of speed vs. stopping distance. They will notice that the second differences are approximately constant and conclude that the function must be quadratic. The subsequent discussion includes consideration of why this assumption is reasonable in terms of the situation, as well as a brief review of the concept of proportionality.

Approximate Time

20 to 25 minutes for activity (at home or in class)
10 to 15 minutes for discussion

Classroom Organization

Small groups or individuals, followed by whole-class discussion

Doing the Activity

Based on their work in *Quadratic Tables*, students will probably recognize that the data set can be represented by a quadratic function, because the second differences are approximately constant. (They are mostly 2.8, with an occasional 2.7. The fact that they are not constant is accounted for by the distances having been rounded off to the nearest tenth.)

Students may be stuck when it comes to finding a specific quadratic function that fits the data set. It turns out that the best fit comes from a function that is "pure quadratic"—that is, a function with only an x^2 term.

One approach you might take if students need assistance is simply to tell them to try a function of this form. Here are some other approaches:

- Let students experiment with guess-and-check. (This may not be very productive.)
- Ask what the stopping distance is if the speed is zero. This may suggest to students that the constant term should be zero.
- Help students see that doubling the speed seems to quadruple the stopping distance. This suggests that the function might be pure quadratic.
- Suggest students use the general expression for the second difference, $2ah^2$ (which may have arisen following the discussion of *A General Quadratic*). They can use the facts that $h = 5$ and that the second difference is approximately 2.8 to get $2a \cdot 5^2 \approx 2.8$, which gives $a \approx 0.056$. Once they have a, there are various ways to proceed.
- In the discussion that follows, the subsection "Why Quadratic? A Situation-Based Explanation" explores why stopping distance should involve a quadratic function. You can help students build on those ideas to see that, in fact, the function should have only an x^2 term.

Discussing and Debriefing the Activity

Ask volunteers for their methods of finding the family and the equation. Students presumably will see that the second differences are approximately constant and conclude that the function is quadratic (but see the subsection "The Converse of Constant Second Differences" in the discussion of *A General Quadratic*).

If you told groups to look for a function with only an x^2 term or in some way suggested that the function ought to have this form, they may have simply used one of the pairs in the table as values for x and y to get a value for the coefficient. For instance, using $x = 25$ and $y = 34.7$ would produce the equation $34.7 = a \cdot 25^2$. The pairs all give values between 0.055 and 0.056.

You may want to bring out that if we know the function has the form $y = ax^2$, we need only one accurate point, other than (0, 0), to find a.

If students used the expression $2ah^2$ for the second difference and got $a \approx 0.056$, they might either see how close the function $f(x) = 0.056x^2$ is to the data items (very close!) or use guess-and-check or substitution of specific points to find the other coefficients.

In any case, students should get a function such as $f(x) = 0.056x^2$ [or, slightly better, $f(x) = 0.0555x^2$] for the data items in the table.

Why Quadratic? A Situation-Based Explanation

If you haven't yet done so, ask the class to consider this question: Why, in terms of the situation, should the stopping distance be expressible as a quadratic function? In other words, is there some explanation, separate from the specific data set, that would lead us to expect a function of this form?

Any explanation should be based in some way on the assumption that the car decelerates at a fixed constant rate—that is, at the same rate no matter what the initial speed. (This is a reasonable assumption. If this is not the case, the data set will probably not be quadratic.)

Here is one possible explanation. Because the rate of deceleration is a fixed value, we get these two consequences:
- The time it takes for the car to stop is a linear function of the initial speed.
- The car's average speed while it is stopping is a linear function of the initial speed.

The distance the car travels is the product of the time and the average speed—that is, a product of two linear functions. Therefore, the distance is a quadratic function. This reasoning shows, more specifically, that the function is *pure quadratic*, because each of the two factors just described is *pure linear*.

Stopping Distance Is Proportional to the Square of Initial Speed

Whatever explanations students (or you) offer, be sure to state the conclusion clearly. It might be summarized by this statement:

If the rate of deceleration is fixed, then the distance required for the car to stop is proportional to the square of the car's initial speed.

The fact that the stopping distance is proportional to the square of the initial speed means, for instance, that doubling the initial speed quadruples the stopping distance, that tripling the initial speed multiplies the stopping distance by 9, and so on. If the class has not previously made this type of observation about the data set in the table, raise it yourself.

You may also want to have students test out functions other than pure quadratic to see that none of them has the property that doubling the input always quadruples the output.

Two Types of Reasoning

Point out that students have seen two very different routes to the conclusion that the stopping distance is proportional to the square of the car's speed:
- By direct observation of the data set
- By reasoning based on the nature of the situation

Both approaches can be useful in deciding what type of function should be used in a given situation. Remind students that choosing the type of function to describe a situation is an example of *mathematical modeling* and is an important component of the process of analyzing a situation mathematically. Also mention that whether students first look at the data set or first try to reason directly in terms of the situation, it's usually a good idea to try to work the other way as well for confirmation.

Looking Ahead to a Variation on the Problem

Point out that the data set in *Brake!* ignores the fact that some time elapses between when a driver sees an emergency requiring him or her to stop and when the driver hits the brakes. From a safety point of view, the more important question is how far the car travels from when the driver sees the emergency until the car stops. Tell students they will explore this idea at the end of the unit (in the activity *Better Braking*).

Key Question

Why, in terms of the situation, should the stopping distance be expressible as a quadratic function?

Bigger Means Smaller

Intent

This activity introduces the concept of inverse variation.

Mathematics

In this activity, students encounter the concepts and vocabulary of inverse and direct proportionality. They also consider the family of reciprocal functions.

Progression

The teacher introduces this activity with a brief discussion of proportionality. Students then explore situations involving inverse proportionality. The follow-up discussion introduces the terms *inversely proportional*, *inverse variation*, and *directly proportional,* and the class adds the family of reciprocal functions to their poster and notes.

Approximate Time

5 to 10 minutes for introduction
20 to 25 minutes for activity (at home or in class)
10 to 15 minutes for discussion

Classroom Organization

Individuals, followed by whole-class discussion

Doing the Activity

In the discussion of *"Brake!" Revisited*, students saw that the car's stopping distance is proportional to the square of the car's initial speed. This provides a good opportunity to review what they learned in previous units about proportionality. You might begin by asking, What other situations have you seen in which one quantity is proportional to the square of another?

The topic of area provides some examples. For instance, students know that the area of a circle is proportional to the square of its radius. (You may want to review the term *constant of proportionality*.)

Also ask for examples of "simple" (that is, linear) proportionality—namely, situations in which something is simply "proportional to something else" rather than "proportional to the *square* of something else." These examples can be as basic as seeing that the price of a watermelon is proportional to its weight. Students might also mention the calculator-purchase situation from Question 1 of *Back to the Basics*.

Discussing and Debriefing the Activity

Questions 1 and 2

Questions 1a and 1b and Questions 2a and 2b should be straightforward. The equations in Questions 1c and 2c may take a bit of discussion, but students will likely be comfortable with these as well. They should get an equation equivalent to $L = \dfrac{43,560}{w}$ for Question 1c and to $t = \dfrac{300}{s}$ for Question 2c. Save these two equations for use when you introduce *Don't Divide That!*

Question 3

In the discussion of Question 3, students should articulate that in both cases, the *Out* was found by dividing some fixed number by the *In*. Let several students share their ideas about this. You may get a variety of ways of articulating the idea that as one variable goes up by some factor, the other goes down by the same factor.

Introduce the term *reciprocal function family* for the set of functions of the form $f(x) = \dfrac{K}{x}$ for some constant K, and add this family to the class poster. Make sure students know what *reciprocal* means.

Also introduce the term *inversely proportional,* and tell students that the phenomenon illustrated in Questions 1 and 2 is called *inverse variation*. Explain that "inverse" here means essentially the same thing as "reciprocal."

It would be helpful to illustrate different ways in which the terminology of inverse variation is used. For example, we can describe the situation in Question 1 with statements like these:
- "The length of the field varies inversely to the width."
- "The length of the field is inversely proportional to the width."
- "The length of the field is proportional to the inverse of the width."

Ask students to come up with similar statements for Question 2, such as these:
- "The time of the trip varies inversely to the speed."
- "The time of the trip is inversely proportional to the speed."
- "The time of the trip is proportional to the inverse of the speed."

Point out that with inverse variation, one variable gets smaller when the other gets bigger (hence the title of the activity). But be sure students recognize that not every situation in which variables move in opposite directions involves inverse variation. For example, in Question 4 of *Back to the Basics*, Chloe's vacation money decreased as the number of vacation days increased, but this situation does not represent inverse variation. (It's simply a linear function with negative slope.)

Tell students that we use the term *directly proportional* to explicitly distinguish situations of the sort discussed when introducing this activity (such as the price of a watermelon) from situations involving inverse proportionality. That is, we might say, "The price of a watermelon is directly proportional to the weight of the watermelon." (And if you have a fixed amount of money to spend, the amount of watermelon you can buy is inversely proportional to the price per pound of watermelons.)

Key Questions

What are similar statements you can use for Question 2?
What other situations have you seen in which one quantity is proportional to the square of another?

Going to the Limit

Intent

In these activities, students explore the related concepts of asymptotes and the end behavior of a function.

Mathematics

The activities begin with the introduction of asymptotes. Students look at what causes vertical and horizontal asymptotes, both with respect to the algebra of a function and with respect to the situation from which the function arises. They then explore the end behavior of functions.

Progression

Don't Divide That! introduces the idea of asymptotes. In *Difficult Denominators*, students see that it is possible for a function to have multiple asymptotes, and they look at variations in the possible behavior of a function as it approaches the asymptote. They consider the meaning of vertical asymptotes in the context of the problem situation in *Return of the Shadow*, where they also learn of the family of rational functions, and do the same for horizontal asymptotes in *An Average Drive*.

Approaching Infinity provides reference material on the basic ideas and notation related to end behavior of functions. In *The End of the Function*, students identify the end behavior of various functions, and in *Creating the Ending You Want*, they find functions with given end behaviors.

Don't Divide That!
Difficult Denominators
Return of the Shadow
An Average Drive
Reference: Approaching Infinity
The End of the Function
Creating the Ending You Want

Don't Divide That!

Intent

Students identify the phenomenon of vertical asymptotes.

Mathematics

Students explore the issue of division by zero in the context of graphs and are introduced to the notion of vertical asymptotes.

Progression

In their groups, students examine the relationship between multiplication and division to explain why division by zero is undefined. They then explore two functions that have x-values that make the denominator equal to zero. Their exploration leads into a discussion of vertical asymptotes.

Approximate Time

40 minutes

Classroom Organization

Small groups, followed by whole-class discussion

Doing the Activity

Have students look at the equations for Questions 1c and 2c of *Bigger Means Smaller* ($\ell = \dfrac{43,560}{w}$ and $t = \dfrac{300}{s}$, respectively). Point out that equations with variables in the denominators create potential complications for substitution.

Then have groups look at Part I in this new activity. They need only discuss the issue—no written work is expected.

Before they move to Part II, explicitly point out that they are to make sketches by hand before graphing on their calculators, and ask, What are some possible reasons why you are asked to draw the graph by hand first? The issue can be discussed after the activity as well. Here are two reasons that might be raised, now or later:

- You never see the whole graph on a calculator. Therefore, you need some other way to figure out what to look for so you'll know what window settings might be useful.
- Calculators sometimes do funny things in connection with division by zero and may even give misleading graphs.

Discussing and Debriefing the Activity

Let one or two groups share ideas about Part I.

Once the key ideas are articulated, have one or two other groups present work on Part II. Ask them to focus on what happens near the values where the denominator is zero ($x = 0$ for Question 1 and $x = 3$ for Question 2) and to justify their graphs by talking about specific values.

For example, in Question 2, presenters should discuss the value of y if x is something like 2.9 or 3.001. Be sure they consider the sign of the denominator. For instance, the graph of Question 2 is "very negative" if x is slightly greater than 3 (because $3 - x$ is negative) and "very positive" if x is slightly less than 3 (because $3 - x$ is positive).

Asymptotes

Introduce the term *vertical asymptote* to describe the line $x = 3$ in relation to the graph of Question 2. *Asymptote* is not defined formally in the student book, as that would involve a discussion of the concept of limit. Instead, explain informally that an **asymptote** of a graph is some line that the graph approaches more and more closely, and demonstrate with an example.

Ask students, Does the graph in Question 1 have a vertical asymptote? They should see that the y-axis itself is a vertical asymptote for this graph. What is its equation? This will remind students that the y-axis is the graph of the equation $x = 0$.

Can you see any lines that might be considered asymptotes for either of these graphs, other than the two vertical asymptotes just discussed? If needed, ask if there are any other lines that the graph gets closer and closer to. Students should see that both graphs get close to the x-axis as x gets very big (both "positive big" and "negative big"). They can probably guess that these lines are called *horizontal asymptotes*.

Asymptotes on the Calculator

Ask students, What did you notice when you graphed the functions on your calculators? They likely got a graph like this, showing the vertical asymptote as if it were part of the graph itself:

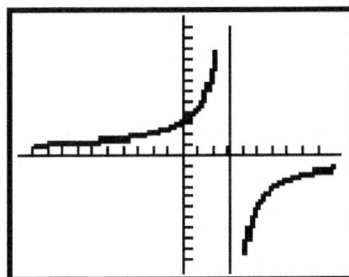

This phenomenon provides an opportunity to begin or resume the discussion of why it's important to be able to sketch a graph without a calculator.

You may also want to discuss how students decided on their window settings and the variations that occurred as they changed the settings.

Asymptotes and the Problem Situations

Now ask students, *What asymptotes do the graphs of the functions in Bigger Means Smaller have?* They should see that both graphs have the vertical axis as a vertical asymptote and the horizontal axis as a horizontal asymptote.

What do those asymptotes mean in terms of the problem situations? For example, students can interpret the vertical asymptote in Question 2 as illustrating that as the speed of the car gets closer to 0, the time required for the trip gets very large. The horizontal asymptote illustrates what happens as the car's speed increases.

Key Questions

What are some possible reasons why you are asked to draw the graph by hand first?
Does the graph in Question 1 have a vertical asymptote? What is its equation?
Can you see any lines that might be considered asymptotes for either of these graphs, other than the two vertical asymptotes just discussed?
What did you notice when you graphed the functions on your calculators?
What asymptotes do the graphs of the functions in Bigger Means Smaller have?
What do those asymptotes mean in terms of the problem situations?

Difficult Denominators

Intent

This activity focuses on the behavior of graphs near vertical asymptotes.

Mathematics

Continuing their work with vertical asymptotes, students see that a function may or may not have a change in *y*-values symmetrically about a vertical asymptote and that a function may have multiple asymptotes.

Progression

Students continue to explore vertical asymptotes, including looking at a function for which the *y*-value becomes infinitely large on either side of an asymptote and a function that has two vertical asymptotes.

Approximate Time

30 minutes for activity (at home or in class)
10 minutes for discussion

Classroom Organization

Individuals, followed by whole-class discussion

Doing the Activity

This activity requires no introduction.

Discussing and Debriefing the Activity

Give students a few minutes to compare their graph sketches in their groups. Then have students from different groups present their results.

Question 1 is a fairly straightforward review of the ideas from *Don't Divide That!*
The graph looks like this:

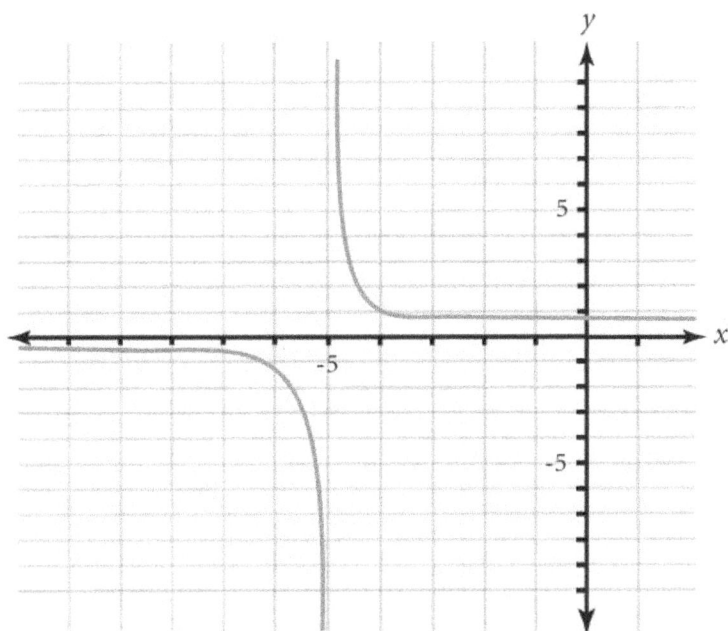

For Question 2, when students substitute values near $x = 2$, they should see that the y-values are positive on both sides of the vertical asymptote. Here is a sketch of the graph:

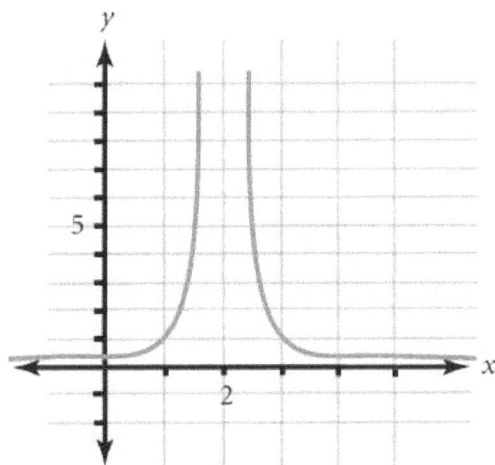

To more clearly focus on the issue of sign, you might ask, **What would the graph of the equation** $y = \dfrac{1}{(x-2)^3}$ **look like?**

The basic issue in Question 3 is the presence of two vertical asymptotes. Substitution of values near $x = 5$ and $x = -5$ should clarify the behavior of the graph near the asymptotes.

Students may be unsure what happens to the graph as the absolute value of *x* gets very large. As with vertical asymptotes, substitution of numeric values (for instance, *x* = ±1000) should help. This issue is explored further in *The End of the Function*.

Here is a graph for the function:

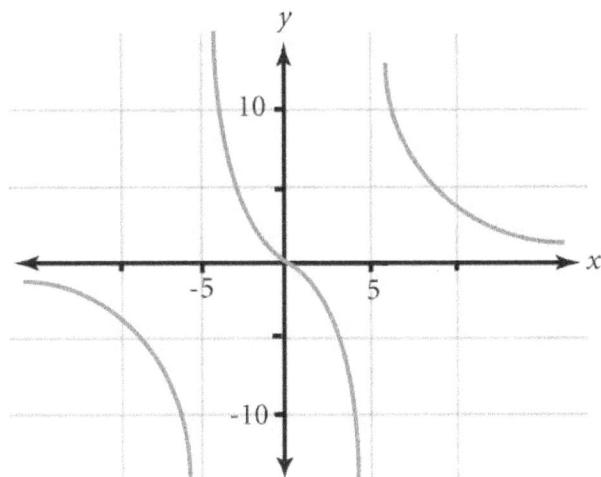

Key Question

What would the graph of the equation $y = \dfrac{1}{(x-2)^3}$ look like?

Return of the Shadow

Intent

Students investigate the meaning of asymptotes in a real-world context.

Mathematics

Looking at the relationship between the height of an object and the length of its shadow, students review ideas about similarity and develop a rational function for the relationship, introducing them to that family of functions. They then explore the issue of why the graph of the function has an asymptote, both in terms of the algebra of the function and in terms of the problem situation.

Progression

Students find an expression for the length of the shadow in a specific situation as a function of the height of the person casting the shadow and then examine whether this relationship is a direct proportionality. (They should discover that it is not.) The subsequent discussion introduces the family of rational functions and then focuses on the issue of why the function's graph has an asymptote.

Approximate Time

35 to 40 minutes

Classroom Organization

Small groups, followed by whole-class discussion

Doing the Activity

Have students read the activity. Discuss it briefly as a class before groups begin work, emphasizing these points:

- One main question posed is whether shadow length is proportional to height.
- Students should use the specific case given—lamppost height of 20 feet and distance from the lamppost of 12 feet—as the basis for answering this question.

As a first step, groups should draw a diagram of the situation, which will look something like this:

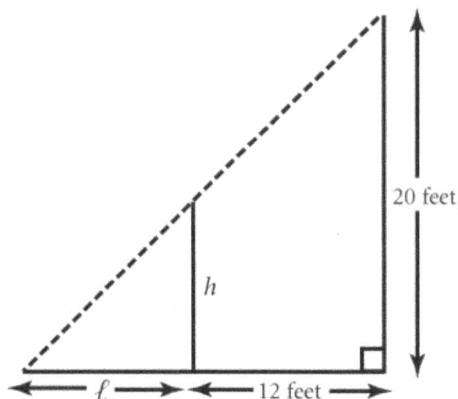

They then might compare the small triangle to the large triangle, get the proportion equation

$$\frac{\ell}{h} = \frac{\ell + 12}{20}$$

and find ℓ in terms of h. (Some students may need a quick review of similar triangles.)

Even after multiplying both sides of this equation by $20h$, some students may need assistance in moving from the equation $20\ell = h(\ell + 12)$ to an expression for ℓ in terms of h. Some might find it helpful to try specific numbers for h and see how ℓ is found in each case. Another approach is to compare the small triangle to the similar triangle in the upper right that is shaded in this diagram:

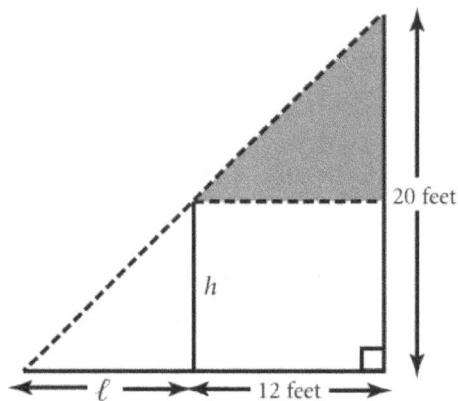

This gives the following equation, which can be multiplied by h on both sides to give ℓ in terms of h:

$$\frac{\ell}{h} = \frac{12}{20 - h}$$

Discussing and Debriefing the Activity

Let two or three students present their ideas on getting ℓ in terms of h. They will probably end up with the equation

$$\ell = \frac{12h}{20 - h}$$

Then say, **Suppose Emily is 2 feet, 8 inches tall. Use your equation to compare the length of her shadow to the length of her mother's shadow.** Students should see that the mother's shadow is more than twice as long as Emily's. **Can anyone explain why this is so from the form of the function?** Help students understand that this means that shadow length is *not* proportional to height.

The Family of Rational Functions

Point out that both the numerator and denominator of the fraction are polynomials, and explain that functions that are quotients of polynomials are called **rational functions**. You may want to compare this term to the phrase *rational number*.

To verify that students understand the definition, ask, **Can you make up other examples of rational functions?**

Have students add the *rational function family* to the poster and their own lists. Point out that reciprocal functions (such as those used in *Bigger Means Smaller*) are a special kind of rational function.

The Shadow Function Asymptote

Now ask, **What do you think the graph of this function will look like?** Have students use their calculators to graph the function. They may not think about the window settings initially, and that may lead to some interesting observations. Be sure to have them look at a window setting that includes the value $h = 20$, and discuss what happens there. They should identify the line $h = 20$ as a vertical asymptote for this function.

Why does this graph have an asymptote? Make sure to get explanations in terms of both the algebraic form of the function and the problem situation.

- The algebraic form of the function: Students should recognize by now that there is a vertical asymptote at $h = 20$ because that value makes the denominator equal to zero. More specifically, as h increases toward 20, the fraction $\dfrac{12h}{20 - h}$ gets very large.

- The problem situation: Ask students what would happen to the length of a person's shadow if the person grew taller. They should see that if a person grew toward a height of 20 feet, that person's shadow would get very long, at least according to this model of the situation.

This graph also has a horizontal asymptote at $\ell = -12$ as h increases in absolute value (in either direction). That asymptote is not mentioned here because the situation doesn't make sense for values of h with large absolute value (either positive or negative). *An Average Drive* includes a more meaningful example of a horizontal asymptote, and the discussion of that activity does include an examination of how the asymptote relates to the problem situation.

Key Questions

Can you make up other examples of rational functions?
What do you think the graph of this function will look like?
Why does this graph have an asymptote?

An Average Drive

Intent

Students develop an equation that involves a horizontal asymptote.

Mathematics

This intriguing activity will be the basis for a discussion of how a horizontal asymptote might be interpreted in terms of a problem situation.

Progression

Students analyze a problem situation to develop an expression that creates an equation with a horizontal asymptote. After discussing the solutions, the class graphs this function and discusses the meaning of both the vertical and the horizontal asymptotes in terms of the situation. Finally, the class reviews other functions with horizontal asymptotes and looks at how those asymptotes can be explained in terms of the problem situations.

Approximate Time

20 to 25 minutes for activity (at home or in class)
15 to 20 minutes for discussion

Classroom Organization

Individuals or small groups, followed by whole-class discussion

Doing the Activity

Make sure students understand that the average speed mentioned in the activity is for Amparo's trip to the beach *and* back.

Discussing and Debriefing the Activity

A common error on Question 1 is to reason that because the average of 60 and 40 is 50, the answer is 40 mph. Make sure students understand why this is incorrect. Ask for a volunteer who got an answer other than 40 mph to explain the reasoning.

One method is to consider the travel times involved. The reasoning might go like this: The overall trip is 200 miles, which means that to average 50 mph, Amparo must complete the round trip in 4 hours. She averages 60 mph while driving the first 100 miles, so the trip to the beach took $\frac{100}{60}$ hours. This leaves 4 –

$\left(\frac{100}{60}\right)$ hours remaining, or approximately 2.33 hours. To travel the 100 miles

home in 2.33 hours, she must average $\frac{100}{2.33}$ mph, or about 42.9 mph. (The exact

value is $42\frac{6}{7}$ mph.)

Question 2 has no answer. Amparo averaged only 25 mph going to the beach, so she used the entire four hours already.

If no one found a general expression for Question 3, you may want to have students explore it in their groups. They might work the problem using specific values of x (greater than 25) and then try to generalize.

Have a couple of students present their expressions. They are likely to get different but equivalent expressions or to use different reasoning.

If students follow the reasoning described for Question 1, they will get $\frac{100}{x}$ for the

amount of time Amparo uses going to the beach, $4 - \frac{100}{x}$ for the amount of time

remaining for the trip home, and thus $\dfrac{100}{4 - \dfrac{100}{x}}$ for the average speed required for

the trip home.

If a student presents the answer in this form, have the class simplify it. This is a good opportunity to get students to articulate the key principle for simplifying fractions: Multiplying numerators and denominators by the same nonzero number leaves the fraction unchanged. The most common simplified forms will likely be

$\dfrac{100x}{4x-100}$ and $\dfrac{25x}{x-25}$. (Strictly speaking, $\dfrac{100x}{4x-100}$ is not equivalent to $\dfrac{100}{4 - \dfrac{100}{x}}$,

because the first expression is defined when $x = 0$ and the second is not. But the value $x = 0$ doesn't make sense in the problem anyway.)

The Graph and the Vertical Asymptote

Once one or more correct versions of the expression have been found for Question 3, have students graph the function on their calculators. With appropriate adjustment of window settings, they should see that the graph has a vertical asymptote for $x = 25$.

Ask, **What does the vertical asymptote mean in terms of the situation?** Students should be able to explain that the closer x is to 25 mph, the faster Amparo has to go on the way back. (The variable x represents her speed on the way to the ocean.) The required return speed becomes very large as her average speed going to the ocean gets closer to 25 mph.

A Horizontal Asymptote

Ask, **Does this graph have any other asymptotes?** Students may think the x-axis is a horizontal asymptote because the y-value is decreasing as x gets large. If so, encourage them to look more carefully, perhaps trying very large values of x, such as $x = 1000$.

They should see that the y-values are actually getting closer to 25 as x gets large. With some help, they should see why this is so in terms of the algebraic expression. For example, they can see that for very large values of x, $\dfrac{100x}{4x - 100}$ is approximately the same as $\dfrac{100x}{4x}$, which is equal to 25.

Thus, the line $y = 25$ is a horizontal asymptote for this function.

What does this asymptote mean in terms of the situation? This is not an easy question, so students may have trouble with it.

One approach is to recognize that there is a symmetry between the speeds in the two directions. That is, if a mph going and b mph returning is a possible pair of speeds, then so is b mph going and a mph returning. Therefore, the vertical asymptote at $x = 25$ is matched by a horizontal asymptote at $y = 25$.

If this is too abstract, you might help students to recognize that as x increases, Amparo has more and more of the 4 hours available for the return trip, so she can slow down to almost 25 mph. But because her trip to the beach must take some nonzero amount of time, she'll never have the full 4 hours for the return trip. Thus, her return speed must always be more than 25 mph.

Horizontal Asymptotes in Previous Problems

Now ask students, **What other functions have you studied that had horizontal asymptotes?** If necessary, remind them of the reciprocal functions they used in connection with *Bigger Means Smaller*. Help them, as needed, to see that the x-axis is a horizontal asymptote for such functions. They should be able to give intuitive explanations for the horizontal asymptote in those situations. For example, as the field in Question 1 gets wider, its length would have to get smaller to keep the total area equal to 1 acre.

You may also want to bring up the case of the "shadow function" from *Return of the Shadow*, defined by the equation $\ell = \dfrac{12h}{20-h}$. Values of *h* greater than 20 do not make sense in the context, so what happens as *h* gets very large may not be that interesting. But students should be able to look at the function separately from its context and see that as *h* becomes very large, the value of ℓ gets closer to −12. That is, the line $\ell = -12$ is a horizontal asymptote.

You might also have students examine the functions from *Difficult Denominators* for possible horizontal asymptotes. The function in Question 3, given by the equation $y = \dfrac{25x}{x^2 - 25}$, may be particularly challenging, because both the numerator and the denominator get large as *x* increases. If *x* is large, the ratio is roughly the same as $\dfrac{25x}{x^2}$, which simplifies to $\dfrac{25}{x}$, so the ratio gets close to 0.

Key Questions

What does the vertical asymptote mean in terms of the situation?
Does this graph have any other asymptotes?
What does this asymptote mean in terms of the situation?
What other functions have you studied that had horizontal asymptotes?

Approaching Infinity

Intent

This introductory, teacher-led discussion illustrates that horizontal asymptotes can derive from expressions other than rational expressions.

Mathematics

Using as an example the function whose limit as x approaches infinity is e, the reference page in the student book introduces the concept of end behavior of functions—that is, the behavior of the functions as x gets very large in absolute value.

Progression

Present the material here in a brief class discussion. The reference page summarizes these fundamental ideas and notation about end behavior. Students may want to refer to this page when they work on *The End of the Function*.

Approximate Time

5 to 10 minutes for discussion

Classroom Organization

Whole-class discussion

Doing the Activity

Begin by asking students, *What do you remember about the expression* $(1 + \frac{1}{x})^x$? If no one remembers that this is part of the definition of e, have students use their calculators to graph the function defined by the equation $f(x) = (1 + \frac{1}{x})^x$ and then trace the graph to see what happens when x gets large.

They should see that the y-values get closer and closer to a value of approximately 2.72. Students may recognize this as the number e. If not, remind them that this is a rounded-off version of e, and introduce the notation $\lim_{x \to \infty} f(x) = e$ to represent the statement that as x gets very large, $f(x)$ gets closer and closer to e.

Also ask, **What happens to the expression when *x* becomes a "large"** *negative* **number?** Use the notation $\lim_{x \to -\infty} f(x) = e$ to express the result. Students can confirm this, approximately, on their calculators.

Explain that the behavior of a function as *x* gets very large in absolute value (in either the positive or negative direction) is sometimes called the function's *end behavior*. You may want to review once again the importance of considering a function's end behavior, because students can't see it in the viewing window of a calculator. They need to determine what will happen by reasoning algebraically or numerically.

Key Questions

What do you remember about the expression $(1 + \dfrac{1}{x})^x$?

What happens to the expression when *x* becomes a "large" *negative* **number?**

The End of the Function

Intent

Students explore the end behavior of various families of functions.

Mathematics

This activity is a natural follow-up to the discussion of horizontal asymptotes, because such asymptotes represent a special case of what can happen to the graph of a function as x gets very large. The main purpose here is for students to recognize that end behavior is an important part of the overall picture of a function. They cannot find out about the end behavior from a calculator graph, because a calculator graph (like any written graph with an infinite domain) shows only part of the picture.

Progression

Working on their own or in groups, students explore the end behavior of polynomial functions of various degrees and then of functions from other families. They share their ideas in a class discussion.

Approximate Time

25 to 30 minutes for activity (at home or in class)
15 to 20 minutes for discussion

Classroom Organization

Individuals or small groups, followed by whole-class discussion

Doing the Activity

Remind students that they may want to refer to *Approaching Infinity* for the notation related to end behavior.

Discussing and Debriefing the Activity

Let students share their ideas. It is more important that they be able to explain particular cases than that they find the most complete generalizations.

For example, they should be able to explain why the y-value for the equation $y = x^3 + 2x^2 - 5x + 14$ becomes large (in the positive direction) as $x \to \infty$ and becomes "large negative" as $x \to -\infty$. It is less important that they generalize this to all polynomials of odd degree.

Creating the Ending You Want

Intent

Students continue to explore the end behavior of functions.

Mathematics

In *The End of the Function*, students start with various functions and find the end behavior for each of them. This activity reverses the process, specifying various end behaviors and asking students to create functions that behave in each of those ways.

Progression

Working in groups or on their own, students examine several possible function end behaviors. For each, they sketch a graph of a function with that behavior, create an algebraic equation that behaves in that way, and explain how they know their equation exhibits that end behavior. They share findings in a class discussion.

Approximate Time

30 minutes for activity (at home or in class)
10 minutes for discussion

Classroom Organization

Individuals or small groups, followed by whole-class discussion

Doing the Activity

Remind students that they may want to refer to *Approaching Infinity* for the notation related to end behavior.

Discussing and Debriefing the Activity

Let one or two volunteers share the graphs and equations they found for the various parts of Question 1. If there are conditions for which no one found a function, you might leave these as unresolved problems.

Then have any students who came up with suggestions for Question 2 share their ideas. If there are end behaviors for which no one can find an equation, you might also leave these unresolved.

You may want to suggest specific types of end behaviors other than those mentioned in Question 1. For instance, have students consider the end behavior of functions like $y = \sin x$ or $y = \dfrac{\sin x}{x}$, which oscillate back and forth across the x-axis as $|x|$ gets large. The second of these has the x-axis as a horizontal asymptote, but the first has no horizontal asymptote.

Note: Because a graph does not have to come from an algebraic equation to be a function, any graph that passes the vertical-line test is the graph of some function. Thus, any end behavior that passes that test is possible.

Supplemental Activity

***Real Domains* (extension)** offers students more experience with the concept of domain.

Who's Who?

Intent

In these activities, students find a specific function within a function family to fit a set of data.

Mathematics

Now that students have identified a wide selection of function families, they begin to look at how to select a particular function from within a family. They are reminded of how they have learned to solve for the parameters for a function by substituting data points into the function and obtaining a system of equations in the variables for the parameters. They are then introduced to regression and the calculator's regression feature. Throughout these activities, students are shown that no matter how well a function fits a set of data, it is not useful unless the situation from which the data are drawn suggests that the associated family of functions is appropriate.

Progression

The first two activities review the process of adjusting parameters to find a specific function that fits several data points: *Families Have Many Different Members* for the exponential family of functions and *Fitting Mia's Birdhouses Again* for the quadratic family. *Mystery Tables II* provides practice in selecting a function family and fitting a function based upon data alone (without context), and *What Will It Be Worth* focuses on the importance of first selecting a function family that is appropriate for the given situation. Finally, *The Decision About Dunkalot* lays the foundation for introducing regression.

Families Have Many Different Members
Fitting Mia's Birdhouses Again
Mystery Tables II
What Will It Be Worth?
The Decision About Dunkalot

Families Have Many Different Members

Intent

Students adjust parameters to find a specific function from a family.

Mathematics

By practicing identifying the parameters for a specific function family, students see the importance of choosing an appropriate family before fitting a function to a data set.

Progression

Working in groups, students identify a function for each of two problem situations. The subsequent discussion highlights the fact that for either linear or exponential functions, two points are all that are needed to determine a member of the family.

Approximate Time

60 to 65 minutes

Classroom Organization

Small groups, followed by whole-class discussion

Doing the Activity

If groups need help starting on Question 1, ask them, *What time should $t = 0$ stand for? In other words, when do you want to start the clock?* Even with this suggestion, they may not think they have enough information to get a function unless they recognize that the situation is inherently one of exponential growth. If necessary, remind them of Question 4 of *Story Sketches* and the fact that we can think of the number of bacteria as being multiplied by some fixed factor for each unit of time.

As groups finish working, you might ask them to prepare presentations.

Discussing and Debriefing the Activity

Question 1

The key to Question 1 is the realization that the growth should be exponential. In this context, the phrase "at this rate" means the number of bacteria is multiplied by a certain factor for each time interval of a given size, not that a certain number of bacteria are added.

Students might try to answer part a by looking at successive 3-hour intervals (such as from 2 p.m. to 5 p.m.), but this will not exactly "hit" midnight. Therefore, they are likely to look for the general function before solving the numeric question. That approach is used here.

Once students recognize that the function has the form $f(t) = a \cdot b^t$, they can substitute 0 for t (assuming they let $t = 0$ represent 2 p.m.) to get $a = 1000$.

They can then use the point (3, 2200) to get the equation $2200 = 1000 \cdot b^3$ and solve to get $b = \sqrt[3]{2.2}$, which is approximately 1.301. Thus, the population at time t is $1000 \cdot (\sqrt[3]{2.2})^t$ (which might also be written as $1000 \cdot 2.2^{t/3}$).

To get the population at midnight, students can evaluate this expression at $t = 10$ (as midnight is 10 hours past 2 p.m.). This yields a result of 13,849 bacteria.

Using 1.301 for $\sqrt[3]{2.2}$ gives 13,892 bacteria. Because the original numbers were only estimates, it makes sense simply to say there are approximately 14,000 bacteria at midnight.

The Exponential and Linear Families

Before going on to Question 2, it will be helpful to review an analogy between linear and exponential functions. Both linear and exponential growth involve a kind of constant rate. But in the linear model, the constant growth rate is an absolute growth rate, while in the exponential model, the constant growth rate is a relative growth rate. This analogy can be viewed in other ways as well.

- The equations for these functions have similar forms: $y = a + bx$ and $y = a \cdot b^x$. These symbolic forms reflect the distinction between additive and multiplicative growth. In both cases, a can be thought of as a "starting point" (namely, the y-intercept for the graph) while b represents a "rate of change."
- For both types of functions, two data points will suffice to determine the function (assuming it's known that the function is in the given family).

These two properties of each family are related. That is, two data points (with different x-values, since we're dealing with functions) are needed in each case because each family involves two parameters, a and b.

Two Points Determine an Exponential Function

This discussion begins with the idea that two points determine an exponential function and then looks at the connection to linear functions. It concludes with the observation that the family of quadratic functions is a three-parameter family, so two points do not determine a quadratic function.

You might begin by asking, *How many data points would you need if you knew your data set was perfectly exponential? Why?* Following are two ways students might think about this question. If they don't mention both approaches, introduce them yourself.

An algebraic approach: In this approach, we treat a and b as variables. That is, we create equations involving these two variables and then solve the equations to find the desired function. The goal here is to review that substituting the coordinates of each data point into the general form of the equation yields an equation with a and b as unknowns. (Students should have a general sense that they need two equations if they have two variables, even if the equations aren't linear. Of course, a pair of nonlinear equations may have more than one solution, but such a system will usually have a finite set of solutions.)

To get started, give the class one point and ask for some exponential functions that go through it, perhaps starting with the special case of a point on the y-axis. For example, ask, *What exponential functions go through (0, 6)?* Students might see that the exponential functions $f(x) = 6 \cdot 2^x$ and $f(x) = 6 \cdot 3^x$ both go through this point. Help them see that for the equation $y = a \cdot b^x$ to go through this point means $6 = a \cdot b^0$, which means $a = 6$.

Then give the class a specific second point and elicit the observation that only one function of the form $f(x) = a \cdot b^x$ goes through both points. For instance, if the second point is (3, 50), then a and b must also fit the equation $50 = a \cdot b^3$. Because students already know a, this second equation determines b.

A graphical approach: You can also help students develop an intuitive sense, based on graphing, for why two points determine an exponential function. Start with a single point, such as (1, 5), and ask students if they can sketch several curves with an exponential shape through that point: *Can you sketch some exponential curves that go through (1, 5)?* They should get a diagram like this one:

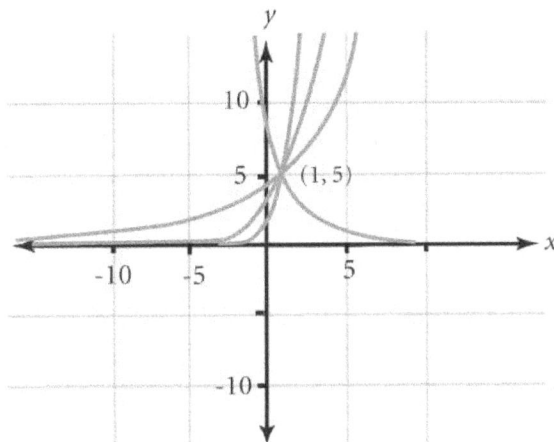

Then add a second point, such as (3, 10), and ask, Which of these curves also goes through (3, 10)? The idea is that this second point determines the "steepness" of the exponential function. To clarify this, help them see that the second point determines the rate of growth for the function. For the specific points (1, 5) and (3, 10), students can see that the y-value must double whenever x increases by 2. The idea of "exponential shape" is not very precise, so connecting this analysis to the context of rate of growth is important.

The Similarity to Linear Functions

Once students have worked with the idea that an exponential function is determined by two points, you can reinforce the similarity between the two "constant growth" families: exponential functions and linear functions.

You might bring out this similarity by asking, What other family (besides the exponential family) has the property that a function in that family is determined by two points? Why? Once this "other family" is identified, explain that this connection has both a geometric basis ("two points determine a line") and an algebraic basis, in terms of the similarity of the forms of linear and exponential functions. Thus, focus on the algebraic analogy between the equations $y = a + bx$ and $y = a \cdot b^x$, as described previously.

Explain that we can refer to each of these two families (linear functions and exponential functions) as a *two-parameter family of functions*. (You may have introduced this term in connection with the discussion of linear functions associated with *Back to the Basics*.)

A Three-Parameter Family

You may want to point out that two points do not determine a quadratic function, because a quadratic function has three parameters: the coefficients *a*, *b*, and *c* in the equation $y = ax^2 + bx + c$. That is, the family of quadratic functions is a three-parameter family.

You can explore this idea using a graphical approach. First have students sketch graphs of quadratic functions that go through (0, 0). Be sure they recognize that there are examples that are not "pure quadratic." Then have them consider those graphs of quadratic functions that also go through (2, 4). The next diagram shows the graphs of the functions $y = x^2$ and $y = 3x^2 - 4x$, two of the infinitely many parabolas that go through both points.

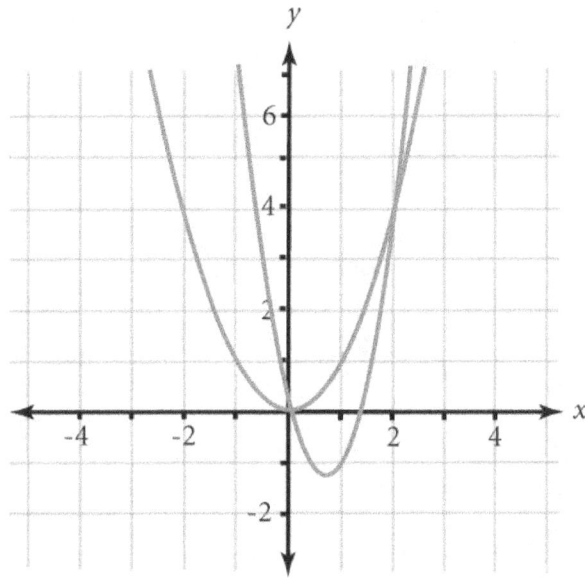

You might also refer back to the activity *Brake!*, where students saw that the function was a very special quadratic, with no linear or constant term. In that case, there was only one parameter, the coefficient of x^2, and one point was enough to determine which function they were looking for.

Question 2

As with Question 1, students are likely to first get a general algebraic expression for the function and then evaluate that expression at the appropriate value for t. They have been given the general form of the function, $f(x) = h_0 + v_0 t - 16t^2$, and know that $h_0 = 200$, so they only need to find v_0.

To find v_0, students must use the fact that the blankets reach the ground after 3 seconds. In other words, when $t = 3$, $h = 0$. This gives the equation

$$200 + v_0 \cdot 3 - 16 \cdot 3^2 = 0$$

This equation simplifies to $3v_0 = -56$, so $v_0 \approx -18.67$ (that is, the blankets are going 18.67 ft/s downward at the instant they're thrown). Thus, the general function for the height after t seconds is given by $h \approx 200 - 18.67t - 16t^2$. Evaluating at $t = 2$ gives $h \approx 98.66$ feet.

Optional: Why Are Two Points Enough?

If you've discussed that the family of quadratic functions is a three-parameter family, you might point out that Question 2 provides only two data points, (0, 200) and (3, 0), and ask, Why are two points enough to determine the quadratic function?

The reason is that this particular situation is only a two-parameter family, because we know the coefficient of x^2 is −16. (This coefficient is based on the strength of the gravitational force.)

Why Quadratic?

Point out that the context for Question 2 explains why the function must be in the quadratic family: the height of falling objects always fits a quadratic expression. Ask, Do the two points (0, 200) and (3, 0) tell you that the function is quadratic? Be sure students recognize that the two data points, by themselves, do not give enough information to determine which family the function belongs to.

You might compare the situation here with the situation in *Brake!* In that activity, the main clue that the situation was quadratic was probably the fact that the second differences were constant. Students had many data points and could investigate in terms of the data set in the table. Only later did they see why that situation was inherently quadratic.

Whether it's the data or the situation that tells us which family to use, it is always wise to look for corroboration from the other point of view. In *Brake!*, it was useful to consider why the context suggested a quadratic function. In the case of a falling body, students could determine the function from only two points, but if they had more points, it would be wise to verify that the additional points also fit the quadratic function.

Key Questions

What time should $t = 0$ stand for? In other words, when do you want to start the clock?
How many data points would you need if you knew your data set was perfectly exponential? Why?
What exponential functions go through (0, 6)?
Can you sketch some exponential curves that go through (1, 5)? Which of these curves also goes through (3, 10)?
What other family (besides the exponential family) has the property that a function in that family is determined by two points? Why?
Why are two points enough to determine the quadratic function in Question 2?
Do the two points (0, 200) and (3, 0) tell you that the function is quadratic?

Fitting Mia's Birdhouses Again

Intent

Students adjust parameters to fit a quadratic equation to a given set of data.

Mathematics

In this activity, a follow-up to finding specific members of a family, students solve a system of equations to find the parameters of a quadratic function. The final question highlights the importance of understanding that the situation needs to fit the chosen function family as well.

Progression

Students plot several data points, find a quadratic function that fits the data, and then consider whether a quadratic function makes sense in the problem situation. They share findings in a class discussion.

Approximate Time

30 minutes for activity (at home or in class)
15 minutes for discussion

Classroom Organization

Individuals, followed by whole-class discussion

Doing the Activity

This activity requires no introduction.

Discussing and Debriefing the Activity

As a first step, have students identify the points they plotted as coordinate pairs: (1, 2), (3, 6), and (5, 8). Then have a volunteer discuss how he or she found a quadratic function to fit this data set.

If students had difficulty with this, have them plot the data set. Then give them a specific quadratic function and ask if it goes through the point (1, 2). Does $y = 2x^2 + 4x + 1$ go through (1, 2)?

Then ask, What would need to be true about the coefficients so that the function would go through this point? Have students go from that work to thinking about what condition on a, b, and c would make the general equation go through that point. **What would have to be true of a, b, and c for the equation $y = ax^2 + bx + c$ to pass through $(1, 2)$?**

Students should see that they can test whether $(1, 2)$ fits such an equation by substituting 1 for x and 2 for y, and evaluating to see if the resulting numeric equation holds true. Thus, the equation goes through the point if and only if $2 = a \cdot 1^2 + b \cdot 1 + c$.

Then have them consider the other two data points. The class should develop a system of three linear equations involving a, b, and c equivalent to this:

$$2 = a \cdot 1^2 + b \cdot 1 + c$$
$$6 = a \cdot 3^2 + b \cdot 3 + c$$
$$9 = a \cdot 5^2 + b \cdot 5 + c$$

If students are seeing this system of equations for the first time now in class, give them some time to work in groups to solve the system. The solution is $a = -\frac{1}{8}$, $b = \frac{5}{2}$, and $c = -\frac{3}{8}$, so the quadratic equation that fits the data is $y = -\frac{x^2}{8} + \frac{5}{2}x - \frac{3}{8}$. Students can check their results by substitution. You might also challenge them to use matrices as another way to check their answers, reviewing the concepts and mechanics as needed.

Have volunteers share their ideas on Question 3. For example, they may point out that because the x^2-coefficient of the quadratic expression is negative, the function would decrease after a while and even become negative. This clearly doesn't make sense in the problem situation.

You might ask, **What type of function would make the most sense simply in terms of the situation?** Students will probably think a linear function would be more reasonable. Point out that they shouldn't discard the idea of using a linear function simply because the data points are not precisely linear.

Key Questions

Does $y = 2x^2 + 4x + 1$ go through $(1, 2)$?
What would have to be true of a, b, and c for the equation $y = ax^2 + bx + c$ to pass through $(1, 2)$?
What type of function would make the most sense simply in terms of the situation?

Mystery Tables II

Intent

This activity offers students more practice finding functions from tables.

Mathematics

This activity is like *Mystery Tables* except that students will also meet functions from the sine family.

Progression

Like its predecessor, *Mystery Tables II* presents tables for six functions and asks students to graph each function, decide which family it belongs to, and find a specific algebraic equation for the function. Several of the functions are in the sine family, presenting an opportunity for discussing how amplitude and period are reflected in a function.

Approximate Time

45 to 55 minutes for activity (at home or in class)
10 to 15 minutes for discussion

Classroom Organization

Individuals, followed by whole-class discussion

Doing the Activity

This activity requires no introduction.

Discussing and Debriefing the Activity

Ask for volunteers to provide equations for the six functions and to explain how they found their answers. How did you get the equations for the six functions?

Students' explanations are likely to refer to the graphs, especially for functions *F*, *G*, and *H*.

Here are the families and possible equations for the first three functions:
- *f* is in the linear family; $f(x) = 2x + 3$
- *g* is in the linear family; $g(x) = 10 - 2x$
- *h* is in the quadratic family; $h(x) = x^2 + 3x - 17$

The functions in the second group are all in the sine family. The equations given here are based on measuring angles in terms of degrees.

- $F(x) = \sin x$
- $G(x) = \sin 2x$
- $H(x) = 2 + \sin x$

You can take this opportunity to talk about period and amplitude in connection with functions F, G, and H. Students may find it helpful to compare H to F.

You might leave any unsolved problems open and offer extra credit for the answers.

Key Question

How did you get the equations for the six functions?

What Will It Be Worth?

Intent

Students compare the effects of various models for growth, including linear and exponential models.

Mathematics

Students explore an example of the consequences of choosing a particular family of functions as a model for a given situation.

Progression

Students work in groups to consider the effects of linear and exponential growth, as well as other models, in the value of a house over 30 years.

Approximate Time

40 minutes

Classroom Organization

Small groups, followed by whole-class discussion

Doing the Activity

Students should be able to do this activity without an introduction.

Discussing and Debriefing the Activity

Ask volunteers for the answers to Questions 1 and 2. (The answers are $175,000 and approximately $283,000, respectively.)

Students may have set up algebraic expressions to get their answers, such as $50,000 + 2500x$ and $50,000 \cdot 1.035x$ (where x is the number of years from 1980). Certainly, they could do Question 1 without such an expression, and they might be able to reason through Question 2 as well by noting that the price doubled in 20 years, so it will be multiplied by $\sqrt{2}$ in 10 years.

If students used x to stand for something other than the number of years from 1980, they will have other expressions in Questions 1 and 2. It may be interesting for the class to explore how the various expressions are related.

Have volunteers share ideas on Question 3. One possibility is a cyclic model, using a function from the sine family. Another is to combine a sine function with a linear or an exponential model.

Then ask students to share their thoughts on Question 4. The intention is for them to realize that the situation is likely to be more complex than any simple model would allow.

Over a long period of time, an exponential model perhaps makes more sense than a linear or cyclic one. An exponential model means the rise in value each year is a certain percentage of the current value, which is like an inflationary model. For instance, one would expect the price of a $100,000 house to rise more than that of a $50,000 house, which would not happen under a linear model. You might also bring out that housing prices will probably never be what they were 20 years ago, so a purely cyclic model—such as a function from the sine family—is not very realistic in the long term (although it may work for short periods).

If students think a linear model is best, ask them how much the house was worth in 1960 under that model. (It would have been worth $0 under a linear model.) Asking about its worth in 1930 would give an even more convincing illustration of the limitations of the linear model, as it would show the house as having been worth a negative amount of money.

Some students may argue that none of the models fits the situation or that the situation is too complex and unpredictable to fit into any single, neat scheme. They are probably right.

The Decision About Dunkalot

Intent

Students consider how to judge whether one function fits a set of data better than another function from the same family.

Mathematics

This activity deals with how to determine a line of best fit. The follow-up discussion introduces the least-squares measurement and the use of regression on the calculator.

Progression

Students examine two possible linear functions to fit a set of data and are asked to judge which fits the data better, to offer a function they believe fits even better, and then to develop a mathematical procedure for making such judgments. The subsequent discussion introduces students to the statistician's tool of looking at the squares of vertical deviations and to the regression feature on their calculators. Students use the regression feature to revisit the data set from *Brake!*

Approximate Time

20 to 25 minutes for activity (at home or in class)
25 to 30 minutes for discussion

Classroom Organization

Individuals, then small groups, followed by whole-class discussion

Doing the Activity

This activity requires no introduction.

Discussing and Debriefing the Activity

Before students discuss their answers, suggest they enter the data set and the two functions given in the activity into their calculators. The four data points and the two graphs look like this:

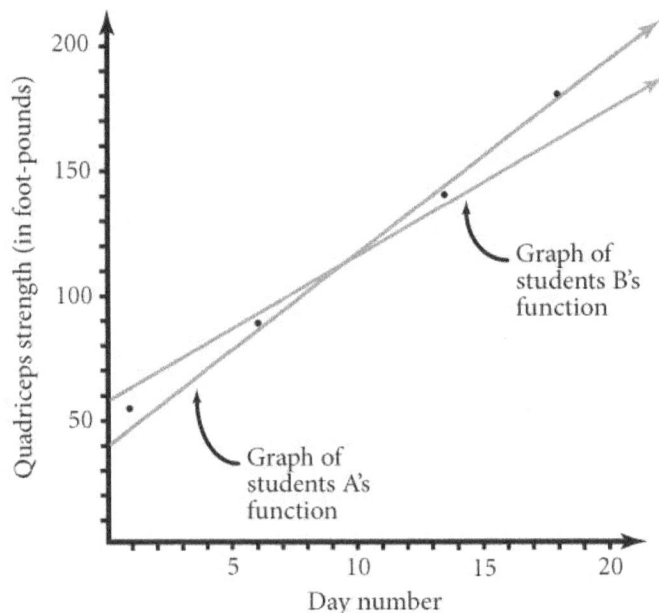

The graph shows "Quadriceps strength (in foot-pounds)" on the vertical axis (marked 50, 100, 150, 200) and "Day number" on the horizontal axis (marked 5, 10, 15, 20), with two lines labeled "Graph of students B's function" and "Graph of students A's function."

Have students discuss answers in their groups and try to decide as a group on a procedure for judging when one approximation is better than another. Then ask members of each group to report on their procedures. There are a number of reasonable possibilities.

One natural approach is to find the *perpendicular* distance from each data point to the graph and then to add these distances. The graph that minimizes this sum could be considered best. A variation is to use the *vertical* distances from data points to the graph. Working with vertical distances makes sense because this measures how far off a prediction based on the graph would be from the actual value. Vertical distances are also easier to find than perpendicular distances.

Tell students that the most common technique is to work with the *squares* of the vertical distances from each data point to the graph. Point out that they saw sums of squares of differences in connection with standard deviation, which is defined using the expression $\sum (x_i - \bar{x})^2$.

Although standard deviation uses sums of squares, it would be reasonable to measure dispersion ("spread-out-ness") of data points instead using the *absolute value* of the difference of each data item from the mean (that is, using the expression $\sum |x_i - \bar{x}|$). But the most common measure involves the squares of these differences. The reasons for that choice (which are somewhat complex) are similar to the reasons statisticians use the **least-squares method** for choosing lines (or curves) of best fit.

Mention that it's possible to draw a graph that goes *exactly* through these four points, and illustrate this idea with a curve. Tell students that when we talk about curve fitting, we are generally looking for a curve from a specific function family.

Tell students that for now, they are to focus on linear functions, that is, functions whose graphs are straight lines. Explain that the line that minimizes the sum of the squares of the vertical distances is called the *regression line* or the *least-squares approximation line*.

Use the Marcus Dunkalot data set to illustrate how the least-squares method works. A chart like this may help:

Day	Actual strength (in ft-lbs)	Strength according to student A's function *f*	Strength according to student B's function *g*
1	55	48	61
6	90	88	91
13	140	144	133
18	185	184	163

Thus, for student A's function, the sum of the squares of the deviations is

$$(48 - 55)^2 + (88 - 90)^2 + (144 - 140)^2 + (184 - 185)^2 = 70$$

For student B's function, the sum of the squares of the deviations is

$$(61 - 55)^2 + (91 - 90)^2 + (133 - 140)^2 + (163 - 185)^2 = 570$$

(Student B's method was far off on that last point!) So, by the least-squares method, student A's function is a better fit to the data set.

Students are free to prefer other procedures for comparing approximations, but they need to know that the least-squares approach is the standard method. One factor in favor of this approach is that the line that minimizes the sum of the squares of the deviations also gives zero for the sum of the deviations themselves. That is, although this line will sometimes predict too high and sometimes too low, adding the positive and negative deviations gives a sum of zero.

Regression

You might want to let students try to get a linear approximation with a lower sum-of-squares of deviations than student A achieved. Otherwise, begin a discussion of how to use the calculator's regression feature.

Students will need to enter the data items and then choose the linear model from the options in the regression menu. In other words, they need to tell the calculator what family they want to look at in trying to minimize the sum of the squares. Identify the use of a linear model as **linear regression.** Similarly, the equation of the line of best fit is called the *regression equation*. The graph of this equation is the *regression line.*

If the linear model uses the form $y = ax + b$, the optimal coefficients are approximately $a = 7.57$ and $b = 45.5$. In other words, the linear function that minimizes the sum of the squares of the deviations is $f(x) = 7.57x + 45.5$. You might have students compute the sum of squares for this function directly. The result is approximately 30—clearly better than student A's result.

The calculator should also provide students with a number, usually labeled r, called the **correlation coefficient.** This is a number between 1 and –1 that measures how well the data set fits the regression line. The closer r is to 1, the better the data set fits a straight line with positive slope. The closer r is to –1, the better the data set fits a straight line with negative slope. The closer r is to 0, the less well the data set fits any line.

For the data in this activity, the value of r is approximately .998. The fact that this value is very close to 1 tells us that Marcus's data set is very close to linear. Substituting 30 for x in the regression equation gives a predicted Cybex test result of approximately 273 foot-pounds, well above the 250 foot-pounds needed for Marcus to return to action safely. Based on this line of best fit, the coach should not put Marcus on the disabled list.

Other Kinds of Regression

Ask students, What other kinds of regression will your calculator do? Point out that they can choose from any of several families and have the calculator find the function from the given family that gives the best approximation to the data set (by the least-squares criterion). The other regression choices probably include these:
- Quadratic: The calculator finds the best quadratic function, using the form $ax^2 + bx + c$, and gives values for a, b, and c.
- Cubic, quartic: The calculator finds the best function of degree 3 or 4, respectively.
- Natural log: The calculator finds the best function of the form $a + b \ln x$.
- Exponential: The calculator finds the best function of the form ab^x.
- Power: The calculator finds the best function of the form ax^b.

The concept of a correlation coefficient is specific to the use of linear regression, although the calculator may provide an analogous value called the *coefficient of determination,* perhaps labeled R^2. As with the correlation coefficient, if this value is close to 1, the function is a "good fit" to the data set.

The calculator may also show a correlation coefficient for some other types of regression, but this is based on transforming the data items. For instance, for exponential regression, the correlation coefficient for the equation $y = ab^x$ is based on the equivalent equation $\ln y = \ln a + (\ln b)x$.

A Perfect Cubic Fit?

Have students try the cubic regression and graph the resulting function, which is defined approximately by the expression

$$0.00840x^3 - 0.156x^2 + 7.73x + 47.4$$

They should find that the associated equation passes exactly through all four points (with reasonable rounding).

Ask, Why does cubic regression give such a good fit? If students are stuck, ask, How many parameters does a cubic function have? Bring out that there are four parameters, so one would expect to be able to find a cubic function that exactly fits any given set of four points (provided they all have different x-values).

Then ask, Is the function that fits the data set always the best one to use for predicting? They should see that this is not necessarily the case and that they need to consider other criteria in addition to "best fit" for determining which function best models a given phenomenon. Mention that there is no particular reason to think that the improvement in Marcus's quadriceps strength should be cubic. You might also remind students of their experience fitting a quadratic function to the data items about Mia and the birdhouses.

You might follow up by asking, What function would fit the data set best if there were five data points? Students should see that it is usually possible to get a quartic (degree 4) function to fit perfectly.

Regression on the Data from Brake!

The data set from *Brake!* gives another nice illustration of the regression technique. Have students enter the data points from that activity, and then ask, What type of regression should you use for this data set?

They should see that quadratic regression makes the most sense. Based on the form $y = ax^2 + bx + c$, they should get results like these for the coefficients (given here to three significant digits):

$$a = 0.0555 \qquad b = -0.000952 \qquad c = 0.0214$$

Have students compare the resulting function with their own analysis from *"Brake!" Revisited*. They should see that it is almost the same as the function they found there. Bring out that b and c are nearly 0 and that the fact that they are not 0 could be explained by approximations involved in the original data set. It's important that students recognize that the coefficients in a regression equation can be no more reliable than the data points were to begin with.

Key Questions

What other kinds of regression will your calculator do?
Why does cubic regression give such a good fit?
How many parameters does a cubic function have?
Is the function that fits the data set always the best one to use for predicting?
What function would fit the data set best if there were five data points?
What type of regression should you use for the *Brake!* data set?

A Tight Fit

Intent

In these activities, students learn there is more to fitting an equation to a set of data than finding the function that comes closest to the given points.

Mathematics

The main point of this section is driven home in the first activity, *Let's Regress,* where students learn that regression is useful only if the situation suggests a function family. A function from a family not appropriate for the situation may fit the data exactly, but would be useless for predicting behavior apart from those data points.

A couple of other topics are dealt with briefly. *Midnight Express* adds absolute value functions and step functions to students' growing repertoire of function families. *In the Lead* sets the stage for introducing the arithmetic of functions.

Progression

Let's Regress
Midnight Express
POW 4: It's Off to College We Go
In the Lead

Let's Regress

Intent

Students explore the regression feature on their calculators.

Mathematics

Students use the calculator to apply different kinds of regression to two situations. The discussion highlights the principle that regression is useful when we know from the situation which function family is involved, but otherwise may not provide good models.

Progression

Students, working in groups, examine data from two situations. In each situation, they select an appropriate regression model and apply it to obtain a function. The follow-up discussion emphasizes the importance of selecting an appropriate function family by evaluating the situation.

Approximate Time

30 minutes

Classroom Organization

Small groups, followed by whole-class discussion

Doing the Activity

As will be brought out in the discussion, students should be wary about applying regression to data sets from a situation if the situation itself provides no clue as to the appropriate function family. In a sense, this is analogous to "data snooping," which can produce hypotheses worth testing but not valid conclusions.

Caution: For Question 3, students will need to choose a finite set of points from the graph to enter as their data points. If they use the point $(0, 20)$, they will get an error message for certain regression models. For instance, if they try a logarithmic model, they will run into trouble because ln 0 is not defined. They will also have a problem with the power function model, because $a \cdot 0^b$ cannot be anything but 0. They can avoid these problems by choosing a point with a very small, nonzero x-coordinate, such as 0.1. Exponential regression will not give an error message for the data points in this problem, but it can't be used if the y-values are not all positive.

As groups finish, ask them to prepare reports on one or two types of regression that they used in one of the problems.

Discussing and Debriefing the Activity

Ask groups to report on their results.

Question 1

Students may find several options that provide a good fit for Question 1. (The fact that there are only four data points makes it easy to get a reasonably good fit. In fact, cubic regression gives a perfect fit, because the family of cubic functions is a four-parameter family.)

Ask, Are there are any good reasons to prefer one model to another? Discuss the idea that it is reasonable to expect the surface area of the wooden model to be proportional to the square of the length of the model, so a function of the form $y = kx^2$ is probably the best. (The equation $y = 1.6x^2$ comes fairly close to all four points. Quadratic regression yields the function $y = 1.77x^2 - 1.12x + 1.29$, which is a slightly better fit but less satisfactory because it is not a pure quadratic function.)

Question 2

Let several groups each present the result for Question 2 from a different regression model. (Much will depend on how many and which points they used.)

Then ask, How would you choose a regression model here? In this case, there is no way to choose a model simply from the data set given—students would need to know more about human growth to make this choice wisely.

For instance, common sense about human growth suggests that the function should be increasing (as x increases) and reach its maximum as the boy reaches adolescence. A horizontal asymptote at average adult male height would be a good alternative.

Use the discussion to raise the idea that regression is not always a useful tool. In particular, students should be wary about applying regression to data items from a situation if the situation itself provides no clue as to the appropriate function family. Using regression without such a clue is like "data snooping." Although one might get some insights from data snooping, that approach does not provide statistically valid information unless the observations are tested on new data sets. There are likely to be many patterns in any set of sample data, and a pattern that fits a particular sample may not fit the overall population.

Similarly, by trying different function families, one might find a function that fits the particular data set, but that doesn't necessarily mean it has any predictive value. In particular, point out that students were able to find a quadratic function that perfectly fit the data set in *Fitting Mia's Birdhouses Again* and a cubic function that perfectly fit the data set in *The Decision About Dunkalot,* but neither of these functions would be very reliable in predicting other outcomes in the given situations.

Key Questions

Are there are any good reasons to prefer one model to another?
How would you choose a regression model here?

Midnight Express

Intent

Students use absolute value and step functions to model situations.

Mathematics

The two function families introduced in this activity, absolute value functions and step functions, are likely to give students some initial difficulty, both in graphing them and in representing them algebraically. An example of the step function, the greatest integer function, is offered in the follow-up discussion.

Progression

Students make a graph and write a rule for two given situations. In the discussion, they add the families of **absolute value functions** and **step functions** to the class poster and their individual notes. The teacher also introduces the **greatest integer function.**

Approximate Time

25 to 30 minutes for activity (at home or in class)
15 minutes for discussion

Classroom Organization

Individuals, followed by whole-class discussion

Doing the Activity

Choose one or two students to prepare to present their graphs for each of Questions 1 and 2.

Discussing and Debriefing the Activity

Have selected students present their work.

Question 1

For Question 1, the graph should have a V shape. One key observation is that the distance is positive whether t is positive or negative (and the distance is 0 when $t = 0$).

The steepness of the sides of the V will depend on the scales and units used. Students will presumably measure t in hours and d in miles, and the graph might look like this:

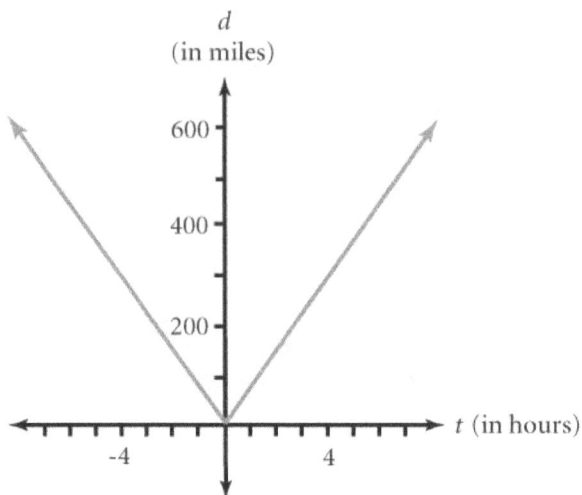

Have volunteers share the rules they found for part b. They might use absolute value, writing $d = |70t|$. Or they might give a verbal description such as, "Multiply t by 70, and make the result positive to find the distance." If students object that this type of verbal description doesn't feel like an appropriate rule, have them describe what they would do for specific values of t, both positive and negative, and then try to put the process into words.

If students do not introduce the use of absolute value on their own, bring it up yourself. You might ask, **What concept represents the magnitude of a number, regardless of sign?**

Have students add the *absolute value function family* to the class poster and their individual lists.

This family does not have a standard definition, so it isn't defined precisely here. One might define it as the set of all functions with V-shaped graphs (opening upward). By that definition, the family consists of all functions of the form

$$f(x) = |ax + b| + c$$

Question 2

Use a similar process to review Question 2, working first with the graph and then with the rule. Use the term *step function* to describe this graph. The graph might look like this:

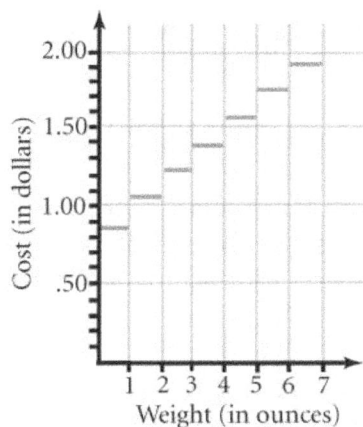

How can you show whether the endpoint of a line segment is included?
Remind students of the convention of using a filled-in circle at the end of a line segment if the point is to be included and an open circle if it is not to be included, as shown in this graph:

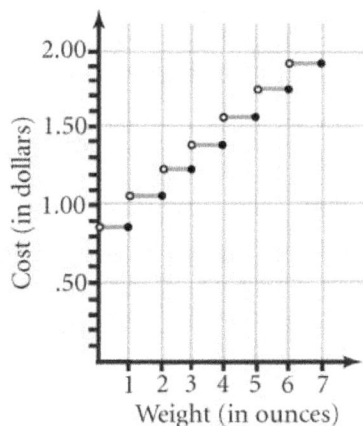

After discussing the graph, ask, **What rule describes this graph and situation?** As with Question 1, you are likely to get verbal descriptions rather than algebraic equations.

Demonstrate the "multiple-definition" method for writing a function of this type. For instance, for weights up to 3 ounces, the function might be defined like this:

$$f(x) = \begin{cases} 88\text{¢ if } x \leq 1 \\ 105\text{¢ if } 1 < x \leq 2 \\ 122\text{¢ if } 2 < x \leq 3 \end{cases}$$

The Greatest Integer Function

Ask, **Does anyone knows a mathematical notation that can be used to help describe the postage function completely (that is, for all values of x)?** If no one does, introduce the *greatest integer function* and its notation. The function is defined as

$$[x] = \text{the largest integer } n \text{ such that } n \leq x$$

Go over some examples to clarify the meaning of the function and the notation, including cases in which x is a positive or negative integer. Make sure students understand that the greatest integer function is not the same as rounding the number to the nearest integer.

Have students draw the graph of the greatest integer function and compare it to the graph of the postage function. They should see a fundamental similarity between the two. They may notice that for the greatest integer function, the open circles appear at the right-hand ends of the horizontal segments that make up the graph. This is the reverse of the situation for the postage function.

Use the term *step function* to describe functions like these. One might define a step function as a function whose graph is a set of horizontal line segments. It isn't required that the segments be of equal length or that the y-values for the segments get larger as x increases, as they do in these two examples.

Finally, ask students, How might you use the greatest integer function to create an equation for the postage function?

This is a bit tricky. Students are likely to try the function $f(x) = 88 + 17 \cdot [x]$, which is almost perfect, but they should see this is incorrect when x is an integer. You might leave this as an open problem. Or you might suggest they try using something like $-[-x]$ to create a graph in which the open circles are at the left-hand endpoints of the segments.

Key Questions

What concept represents the magnitude of a number, regardless of sign?
How can you show whether the endpoint of a line segment is included?
What rule describes this graph and situation?
Does anyone know a mathematical notation that can be used to help describe the postage function completely?
How might you use the greatest integer function to create an equation for the postage function?

Supplemental Activity

***Absolutely Functions* (extension or reinforcement)** provides a further exploration of absolute value functions.

POW 4: It's Off to College We Go

Intent

Students explore the cost of going to college.

Mathematics

This activity presents students with an organizational task that involves many different considerations.

Progression

Students investigate the cost of going to college for four years. Give them about a week to complete this POW, after which they will share their findings.

Approximate Time

5 to 10 minutes for introduction
2 to 4 hours for activity (at home)
30 minutes for discussion

Classroom Organization

Individuals, followed by small-group and whole-class discussion

Doing the Activity

When you introduce the POW, spend some class time brainstorming the various costs students need to consider.

On the day before the POW is due, you might tell students that they will share results in groups (rather than having presentations by a few individuals).

Discussing and Debriefing the Activity

Ask students to share in their groups what they learned about college expenses. You may also want to have a whole-class discussion of what students learned from this activity in terms of mathematics and more general planning skills.

In the Lead

Intent

Students are introduced to the idea of combining functions to create new functions.

Mathematics

This activity introduces the process of subtracting and multiplying functions that fit known situations to get functions to fit new situations.

Progression

Students investigate two questions that require them to combine two functions, the first using the operation of subtraction and the second using multiplication. The subsequent discussion introduces other arithmetic operations on functions, including scalar multiplication.

Approximate Time

20 to 25 minutes for activity (at home or in class)
20 minutes for discussion

Classroom Organization

Individuals, followed by whole-class discussion

Doing the Activity

This activity should require no introduction.

Discussing and Debriefing the Activity

Students will probably find Question 1 fairly straightforward. The function for the distance Speedy covers in t seconds is represented as $m(t)$. Introduce, or have students choose, another letter to represent the function for the distance Sporty covers, such as $s(t)$.

Ask the class, How can you use the notation $m(t)$ and $s(t)$ to express the answers to part a? What about part b? Be sure it's clear that the answer to part a can be written as $m(10) - s(10)$. Students should then see that the answer to part b is $m(t) - s(t)$.

Tell students that mathematicians use the language and notation of ordinary arithmetic for functions as well. In particular, the function describing Speedy's lead in terms of *t* is called the *difference* of the two functions *m* and *s* and is written simply as *m* – *s*.

In other words, the function *m* – *s* is defined by the equation $(m - s)(t) = m(t) - s(t)$, so in this situation, $(m - s)(t) = 0.005t^2 + 0.08t$. This difference function will be used later in the discussion.

Use Questions 2a and 2b to review familiar ideas about exponential and linear growth. Have the class give letter names to the population and electricity-usage functions. For instance, they might write

$$p(t) = 30,000 \cdot (1.02)^t$$
$$e(t) = 5 + 0.2t$$

Then discuss Question 2c. Students should see that the answer is simply the product of the expressions for the two functions. (If students are confused by the switch from *per person* usage to *total* usage, ask how much electricity was used on January 1, 1970. They should see that on average, each of the 30,000 people used 5 kilowatts, for a total of 150,000 kilowatts.)

Point out that the result for Question 2c is similar to that for Question 1b, except that students are multiplying functions instead of subtracting them. Tell them that this new function is called, naturally, the product of *p* and *e*, and is written *p* · *e*. In other words, $(p \cdot e)(t)$ means $p(t) \cdot e(t)$.

Other Operations on Functions

Explain that the other basic arithmetic operations—addition, division, and even exponentiation—can also be defined for functions. Also introduce the idea of multiplying a function by a number. You might illustrate this using the example of the *weekly* per-person electricity usage, which can be expressed as the function 7*e*. That is, 7*e* is the function defined by the equation $(7e)(t) = 7 \cdot e(t)$.

Tell students that the operation of multiplying a function by a number is called *scalar multiplication*. Also mention that the same term is used for multiplying a matrix by a number; you may want to give an example. Explain that in contexts in which numbers are combined with functions or matrices, the term *scalar* is often used as a synonym for *number*.

The Arithmetic of Families

Ask students, What family does the function *m* – *s* from Question 1 belong to? If necessary, have students reconstruct the difference function, $(m - s)(t) = 0.005t^2 + 0.08t$. They should see that the difference function is quadratic, like its "parents."

Ask, **Is the sum and difference of two quadratic functions always a quadratic function?** Make sure students recognize that there are exceptions, in which the quadratic terms cancel out. But the sum or difference will always be an expression of the form $ax^2 + bx + c$—that is, a polynomial of degree at most 2—although some of the coefficients might be 0.

Next, ask, **Which family does $p \cdot e$ (from Question 2) belong to?** If needed, get an explicit statement of the function:

$$(p \cdot e)(t) = 150{,}000(1.02)^t + 6{,}000t(1.02)^t$$

Students should see that this function does not belong to any family they have studied. Explain that combining functions often results in "hybrids" that belong to no standard family.

Tell students that although they have not yet studied all the important families of functions, the rest of their work in this unit will be devoted to looking at ways of combining functions from the families they already know, such as by taking their sums, differences, products, and quotients.

Key Questions

How can you use the notation $m(t)$ and $s(t)$ to express the answers to Question 1a? What about Question 1b?

What family does the function $m - s$ from Question 1 belongs to?

Is the sum and difference of two quadratic functions always a quadratic function?

What family does the function $p \cdot e$ (from Question 2) belong to?

Back to Arithmetic

Intent

In these activities, students use the arithmetic of functions to create new functions from existing ones.

Mathematics

In many situations, relationships cannot be described by functions that fit nicely within one of the common function families. Instead, they require combining two or more functions into something more complex. In these activities, students combine functions using the functions' tables, graphs, and situations.

Progression

The arithmetic of functions is actually introduced through the final activity in the previous section, *In the Lead*. Students follow up the discussion of that activity by using the tables of functions to create tables for combinations of the functions in *The Arithmetic of Functions* and by using the graphs of functions to create the graphs of combinations of the functions in *The Arithmetic of Graphs*. *Back to the Corral* moves back into problems in the context of situations, as students combine a rational function with other functions to fit the situation.

The final activities give students more experience with earlier topics from the unit. Students select a family of functions appropriate for a situation in *Name That Family!* and fit an exponential function to a table of data in *"Small World, Isn't It?" Revisited*.

The Arithmetic of Functions
The Arithmetic of Graphs
Back to the Corral
Name That Family!
Small World, Isn't It? Revisited

The Arithmetic of Functions

Intent

Students examine the tables of functions formed through the arithmetic of functions.

Mathematics

Students use tables of functions to create tables for arithmetic combinations of the functions.

Progression

Presented with two functions that are given only in terms of a table, students make tables for five new functions formed by combinations of those two functions.

Approximate Time

5 minutes for introduction
15 to 20 minutes for activity (at home or in class)
5 minutes for discussion

Classroom Organization

Small groups or individuals, followed (optionally) by whole-class discussion

Doing the Activity

If students need assistance with Question 1, you might ask how they got $(m - s)(10)$ in *In the Lead*, eliciting something like "applied m to 10 and s to 10 and subtracted the answers."

Although the activity mentions the issue of the **domain** for a sum of functions when the individual functions are defined by tables, you may need to clarify that in this activity, the functions in Questions 1 to 5 are defined only for $x = 2$, 3, and 5 because those are the only values listed for x in both tables.

In Question 5, students may be perplexed about what the numerals represent. Clarify that in this context, "1" means the function whose output is always 1, and similarly for "2." Identify these as coming from the **constant function** family. Thus, $h + 1$ means the sum of the function h and the function whose value is always 1. Overall, this means that

$$(h + 1)(k + 2)(x) = (h(x) + 1)(k(x) + 2)$$

Once students get the idea, this activity is quite straightforward.

Discussing and Debriefing the Activity

This activity probably requires no whole-class discussion, except perhaps of ideas about domains.

Supplemental Activities

Odd or Even? **(extension)** introduces the concept of odd and even functions.

Graphing Power **(extension or reinforcement)** focuses on the graphs of power functions.

Ferris Wheel on a Ramp and *Freddie on the Ferris Wheel* **(extension or reinforcement)** involve sums of functions.

The Arithmetic of Graphs

Intent

Students relate arithmetic operations on functions to graphs.

Mathematics

Students work with the graphs of functions to sketch the graphs of sums, differences, and scalar products of functions.

Progression

Students graph the sums, differences, and products of two given linear functions. The subsequent discussion raises the idea that applying addition and multiplication repeatedly to linear functions leads to the family of polynomial functions and that applying all the arithmetic operations to linear functions leads to the family of rational functions.

Approximate Time

5 minutes for introduction
30 minutes for activity (at home or in class)
15 minutes for discussion

Classroom Organization

Individuals, followed by whole-class discussion

Materials

Transparency of *The Arithmetic of Graphs* blackline master

Doing the Activity

To save time in class, as students finish their work (or as you assign it as homework) you may want to ask different students to prepare presentations of Questions 2a, b, and c. If so, ask them to include the graphs of *f* and *g* on the axes they use.

Discussing and Debriefing the Activity

Question 1

Have several students present the different parts of Question 1. The most important is part c, for which students should explain how to use the individual graphs of h and k to create the graph of $h + k$.

For example, the two diagrams here show the graphs of h and k, with dashed-line segments (with arrows) representing the values of $h(-1)$ and $k(-1)$. Explain that the direction of the arrow represents the sign of the value of the function. (If you draw these graphs on a single set of axes, use a different color for each function, and perhaps other colors for the segments themselves.)

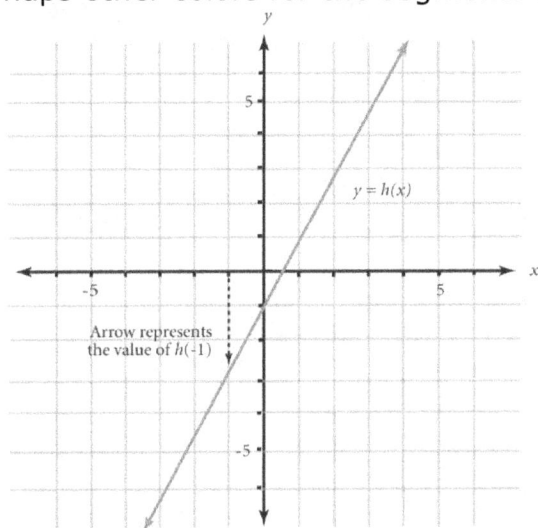

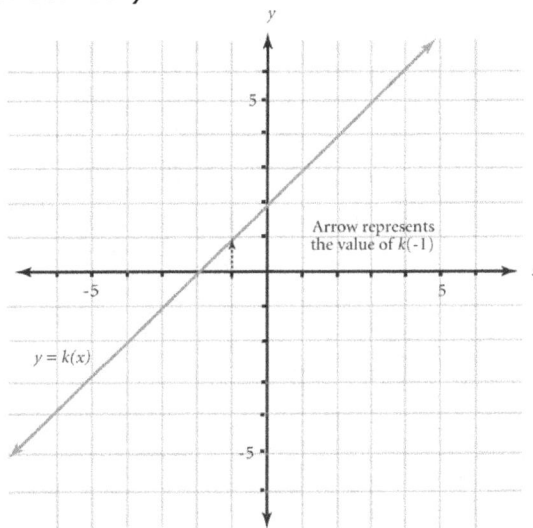

The output for $h + k$ at $x = -1$ [that is, the value of $(h + k)(-1)$] is the sum of the two "directed" segments. The next two diagrams illustrate the idea. The first shows the graphs and the two segments on a single set of axes. The second shows a single segment representing the sum of the two segments. Thus, the endpoint of the arrow in the second diagram is a point on the graph of $h + k$.

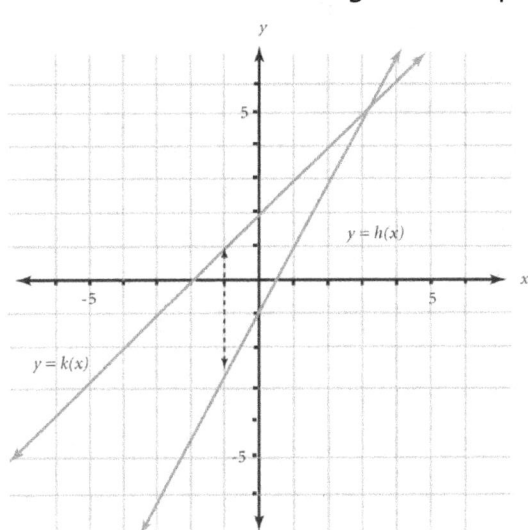

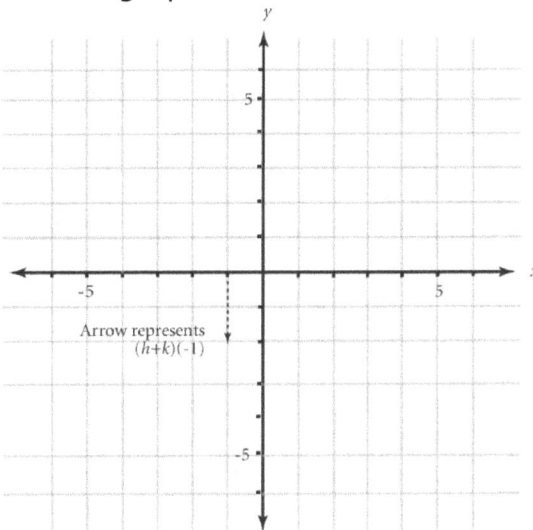

Because $h(-1)$ is negative while $k(-1)$ is positive, we use the difference of the lengths of these segments. Because the segment for h is longer than that for k, the value of $(h + k)(-1)$ comes out negative. (The other examples in Question 1c involve different sign combinations for the two functions.)

Question 2

If students had trouble with Question 1, you might let them work in groups on Question 2 before discussing it.

The main idea in part a is that for each x-value, we simply add the associated y-values. (Make sure students understand that they should not add or subtract x-values.) Students should see that even though there are no coordinates for the points, they can add the heights above (or below) the x-axis to get the y-value for $f + g$.

Students will probably get their new graphs by picking a few representative x-values, finding the related y-values for $f + g$, plotting the results, and then connecting these points with a smooth curve.

For part b, students need to take the difference of the heights. For part c, they simply double the heights.

Question 3

The key idea in Question 3 is that we can't multiply lengths without a scale. To explain this, you might ask, **Based on the diagram, what are possible values for $f(0)$ and $g(0)$?** For instance, students might suggest 6 and −2, respectively. **Where would $(fg)(0)$ be, compared to $f(0)$ and $g(0)$?** Students should see that $(fg)(0)$ would be below the axis, but farther from the x-axis than $g(0)$.

On the other hand, $f(0)$ and $g(0)$ might just as well be 0.6 and −0.2. In this case, $(fg)(0)$ would be closer to the x-axis than $g(0)$, though still below the axis.

The Arithmetic of Polynomial and Rational Functions

Ask the class, **What family do the functions in Question 1 belong to? What about their sum? Does this situation hold in general?** Students should see that the sum of *any* pair of linear functions is either a linear function or a constant function. (In the discussion of *In the Lead,* they saw that the sum or difference of two quadratic functions is usually another quadratic function but could be linear or constant.)

What type of function do you get if you subtract or multiply linear functions? Students should express that like the sum, the difference of two linear functions is also either linear or constant. The product of two linear functions, however, is a quadratic function (assuming we consider a linear function to have an x term, and do not allow $y = k$).

What kind of functions would result if we keep adding, subtracting, or multiplying, starting with linear functions and continuing to expand the "family" to include each new result? Students should see that the result of such operations would always be a polynomial function (introduced in *More Families*).

What kind of functions will you get if you start from linear functions and use all four basic operations, including division? Students should see that the result is the family of rational functions (introduced in *Return of the Shadow*).

Point out that with functions, as with ordinary numbers, when you divide, you need to worry about division by zero. A brief reference to the activities *Don't Divide That!* and *Difficult Denominators* (and also the work on asymptotes) should make this clear.

To put division by zero in context, ask, **What problem situations have you seen that involve dividing functions?** As needed, remind students of their work on *Bigger Means Smaller, Return of the Shadow*, and *An Average Drive*.

Key Questions

Based on the diagram, what are possible values for $f(0)$ and $g(0)$?
Where would $(fg)(0)$ be, compared to $f(0)$ and $g(0)$?
What family do the functions in Question 1 belong to? What about their sum? Does this situation hold in general?
What type of function do you get if you subtract or multiply linear functions?
What kind of functions would result if we keep adding, subtracting, or multiplying, starting with linear functions and continuing to expand the "family" to include each new result?
What kind of functions will you get if you start from linear functions and use all four basic operations, including division?
What problem situations have you seen that involve dividing functions?

Back to the Corral

Intent

Students find a rational function to fit a problem situation.

Mathematics

This activity illustrates the use of rational functions in combination with other functions, giving students another opportunity to work with the arithmetic of functions.

Progression

In their groups, students investigate two situations whose solutions involve rational functions combined with other functions. They share their various solution methods in a class discussion.

Approximate Time

60 to 70 minutes

Classroom Organization

Small groups, followed by whole-class discussion

Doing the Activity

As you circulate, you may notice that students' intuition is that a square is the best solution for Question 1. Insist students justify this answer. They might try various widths and find the corresponding lengths and then perimeters, and then generalize to get an expression for the perimeter in terms of the width. This will produce an equation like $p = 2w + 2 \cdot \dfrac{300}{w}$, which students can graph to find the value of w that minimizes p.

You will likely need to give groups some encouragement as they struggle with Question 2. Again, you might suggest they guess one dimension and figure out what the others must be: Pick a width for the rectangle. What will the length have to be so the area is 300 square feet?

A good place to start is with the rectangle's horizontal dimension, from which students can easily get the radius of the semicircle. (Starting with the rectangle's vertical dimension is much more complicated.) Next, they need to find out how long to make the other dimension of the rectangle to get the desired area, and then find the perimeter. Based on one or two examples, they should develop a general expression for the perimeter in terms of the initial dimension.

On both problems, students will likely use calculators to find the value that minimizes the perimeter function.

You may want to ask groups that finish early to prepare presentations so they will be ready when the other groups are near completion.

Discussing and Debriefing the Activity

Question 1

Students will probably recognize that a square is the most efficient rectangle—that is, the rectangle of area 300 of minimal perimeter. Insist they justify this algebraically, especially because this work can be a model for the more complicated situation of Question 2.

Be sure students see that the expression $2w + 2 \cdot \dfrac{300}{w}$ is algebraically equivalent to $\dfrac{2w^2 + 600}{w}$, so the perimeter function $p(w) = 2w + 2 \cdot \dfrac{300}{w}$ is another example of a rational function.

Question 2

Below is one possible solution to Question 2. You may want to let several groups contribute various steps in the problem's solution. If students had trouble, you might get part of the solution and then let them work from that.

Suppose the rectangle's dimensions are labeled w and v as in the diagram below, so that the radius of the semicircle is $\dfrac{w}{2}$. The rectangle and semicircle will have a combined area of 300, so we need $vw + \dfrac{1}{2}\pi \left(\dfrac{w}{2}\right)^2 = 300$.

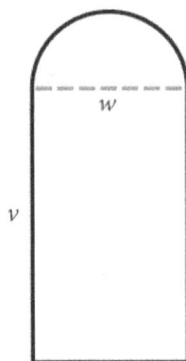

Solving this equation for *v* in terms of *w* gives

$$v = \frac{300 - \frac{1}{2}\pi\left(\frac{w}{2}\right)^2}{w}$$

The perimeter of the figure is given by the equation $p = 2v + w + \pi \cdot \frac{w}{2}$. Substituting the preceding expression for *v* gives

$$p = 2 \cdot \frac{300 - \frac{1}{2}\pi\left(\frac{w}{2}\right)^2}{w} + w + \pi \cdot \frac{w}{2}$$

By examining a graph, students can find that this expression has a minimum when *w* is approximately 18.33, which gives a perimeter of about 65.46 feet. For this value of *w*, we get *v* ≈ 9.17. It turns out that the perimeter is minimized when *v* is exactly half of *w*.

Key Question

Pick a width for the rectangle. What will the length have to be so the area is 300 square feet?

Name That Family!

Intent

Students examine situations to determine the appropriate function families.

Mathematics

The focus of this activity is on identifying the function family appropriate for a given situation. Students sketch graphs to help them make that identification. Most of the graphs involve asymptotes.

Progression

Students examine three situations that describe one variable as a function of another. For each situation, they sketch a graph, name the function family, and explain their reasoning. They share their ideas in a class discussion.

Approximate Time

30 minutes for activity (at home or in class)
20 minutes for discussion

Classroom Organization

Individuals, followed by whole-class discussion

Doing the Activity

This activity does not require an introduction.

Discussing and Debriefing the Activity

Have volunteers explain their work, including any additional assumptions they made in each situation.

Question 1

If students assume each person pulls the same, fixed amount of weeds, regardless of the size of the group, this problem is fairly straightforward and the function is a member of the reciprocal function family. Use the example to review the terminology of inverse proportionality: "The amount of time needed is *inversely proportional* to the number of weeders."

One detail of interest is that this function is discrete. Strictly speaking, its graph is a sequence of individual points rather than a continuous curve. For instance, if the time for one person to do the job were 3 hours, the graph would look like this:

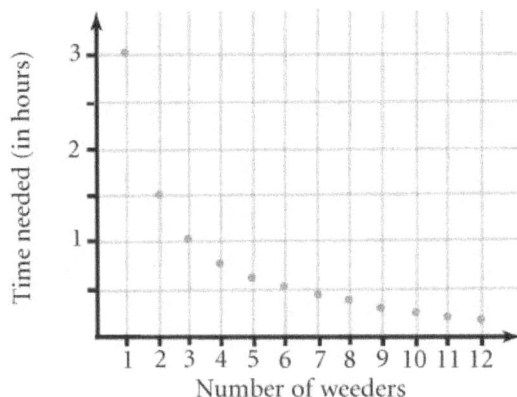

Students may introduce complicating issues, such as distraction caused by workers talking to each other and efficiency limitations due to the number of tools available.

Question 2

Students should be able to get the general shape of this graph, which looks something like the curve below. There is a horizontal asymptote at room temperature, shown by a dashed line (and assuming the room temperature is constant).

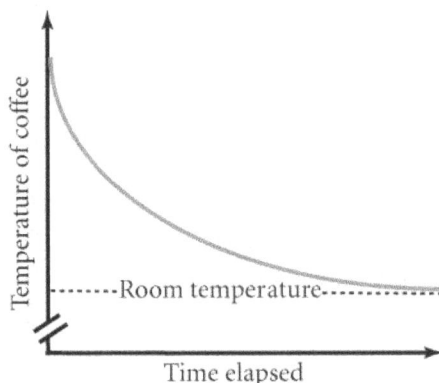

Students may have trouble recognizing the family. Based on the physics principle stated in the problem (and the assumption that room temperature is constant), the function is essentially in the exponential decay family. More specifically, the *difference* between the coffee temperature and the room temperature is an exponential decay function.

You might make an analogy with population growth, with which students are more familiar. If the *increase* in population is proportional to the size of the population, then population growth is expressed by an exponential growth function. Here we are focusing on the difference between the coffee temperature and the room temperature (instead of on population). According to physics, the *decrease* in this temperature difference is proportional to the difference, so it's reasonable that this difference should be an exponential decay function.

Question 3

The intention here is for students to see that the volume is proportional to the cube of the height. If they know the formula $v = \frac{1}{3}\pi r^2 h$ for the volume of a cone, you can bring out that r is some fixed multiple of h. Thus, the function is of the type $v = kh^3$, where k is the proportionality constant.

If students do not know the formula for the volume of a cone, you might ask, **How does the volume of a cube change if its side doubles?** Review the general principle that for any set of similar solid figures, the volume is proportional to the cube of a given linear dimension.

You might connect this situation with Question 1 of *Let's Regress*, in which the surface area of models in a hobby shop was found to be proportional to the square of a given dimension.

Even without developing a specific volume formula, students should see that the graph of volume as a function of height is an increasing function. They should also see that the graph goes through the origin. There are no asymptotes, but the volume "approaches infinity" as the height increases.

Key Question

How does the volume of a cube change if its side doubles?

Small World, Isn't It? Revisited

Intent

Students fit an exponential function to a data set.

Mathematics

In this activity, students will presumably use an exponential function to approximate part of the data set from the Year 3 unit *Small World, Isn't It?* In the supplemental activity *"Small World" Again!,* they apply the tools of this unit to consider all of the data set from the original problem.

Progression

Working from three pairs of data for the population of the world, students estimate the population in 2060, find a general expression that fits the data set, and use the expression to again estimate the population in 2060.

Approximate Time

30 minutes for activity (at home or in class)
10 minutes for discussion

Classroom Organization

Individuals, followed by whole-class discussion

Doing the Activity

This activity requires little or no introduction.

Discussing and Debriefing the Activity

Ask students to share answers in their groups and decide which of their expressions seems to work best. Then have students from one or two groups report.

What is of greatest interest is how students found their expressions and made their predictions. Presumably, they used the assumption that population growth is basically exponential. But the growth percentage from 1960 to 1980 is slightly different from that from 1980 to 2000, so no exponential model will fit the data set perfectly.

Although some students might go straight to the development of a general expression, many will likely start with the numeric problem in Question 1. For example, they might start with these two observations:

- The population went up by a factor of 1.464 from 1960 to 1980.
- The population went up by a factor of 1.369 from 1980 to 2000.

Students might then average the two factors, getting 1.416, and predict growth by a factor of 1.416 for each of the three 20-year periods from 2000 to 2060. This leads to an estimate of 17,290,000,000 (roughly 17.3 billion) as the population for 2060. (Other numeric approaches are possible.)

Question 2 asks for a general expression. Students are likely to use $t = 0$ to represent 1960 and get the population as a function of t. Here are two ways they might build on this labeling in developing a general expression:
- They might start with the form of the function, which can be written as

$$p = a \cdot b^t$$

Substituting 0 for t and 3,040,000,000 for p gives $a = 3,040,000,000$. They might then substitute a second data point, such as 20 for t and 4,450,000,000 for p, to get

$$4,450,000,000 = 3,040,000,000 \cdot b^{20}$$

and solve for b ($b \approx 1.019$). Thus, the general equation is

$$p = 3,040,000,000 \cdot (1.019)^t$$

- Students might essentially treat a 20-year interval as the unit of time. Working again with the 1960 and 1980 populations, this would give an equivalent equation that looks like

$$p \approx 3,040,000,000 \cdot (1.464)^{t/20}$$

Both of these approaches ignore the population given for the year 2000. Students will have to decide how to take all three data points into account.

Once students have found an equation for the function, they can evaluate it at $t = 100$ to answer Question 3.

Point out that the function just discussed does not fit the data set exactly and that no exponential function can. An important aspect of some real-world applications is finding a function that fits data sets *approximately*.

Other approaches may come out that do not reflect an exponential analysis. For instance, students might use a "second difference" analysis that would be appropriate for a quadratic. Because there are only three data points, it is possible to find a quadratic function that fits this data set perfectly.

The point is that students may use methods that are not consistent with the natural assumption that population growth is exponential. The exponential model is not necessarily the best, but help students understand that it makes much more sense in terms of population growth than a quadratic model.

Composing Functions

Intent

In these activities, students explore the composition of functions.

Mathematics

The activities in this section introduce *composition,* an operation on functions in which the output from one function is used as the input for another. This leads into a study of inverse functions.

Progression

The composition of functions is illustrated in *Rumble, Grumble* and *The Cost of Pollution*. The discussion of the former activity defines the concept of composition and introduces the associated notation. Students see how composition is reflected in graphs and tables in *The Composition of Functions*.

Order Among the Functions reveals that composition of functions is not commutative. Students work more with the mechanics of composition in *Cozying Up to Composition* before looking at the decomposition of functions in *Taking Functions Apart*.

Functions in Verse leads to a formal definition of the inverse of a function, after students find some inverse functions and consider the relationships of domain and range of functions and their inverses in *Fish, Ladders, and Bacteria. Linear Functions in Verse* explores the algebra of inverse functions, and *An Inventory of Inverses* highlights their two-sided nature.

Rumble, Grumble
The Composition of Functions
The Cost of Pollution
Order Among the Functions
Cozying Up to Composition
Taking Functions Apart
Fish, Ladders, and Bacteria
Functions in Verse
Linear Functions in Verse
An Inventory of Inverses

Rumble, Grumble

Intent

Students are introduced to the composition of functions.

Mathematics

Students work intuitively with a situation that involves the composition of functions. The follow-up discussion defines *composition of functions* and introduces composition notation.

Progression

Students examine a contrived situation that illustrates the concept of composition of functions. The subsequent discussion names the functions involved so that the composition of functions can be made explicit. It defines composition and introduces associated notation. A function machine diagram helps illustrate the concept.

Approximate Time

10 to 20 minutes for activity (at home or in class)
15 to 20 minutes for discussion

Classroom Organization

Small groups or individuals, followed by whole-class discussion

Doing the Activity

You may want to acknowledge that the situation is a bit contrived, but ask students to do their best with it.

Discussing and Debriefing the Activity

Have one or two students share their ideas. The important idea is how David's hunger level and mood act as intermediate variables between time and Karla's feelings.

For instance, starting at midnight, with David slightly hungry, Karla's feelings are mostly positive. As the night goes by, David gets hungrier. As he gets hungrier, he gets grouchier, and as he gets grouchier, Karla's feelings get less positive. (This assumes they are together 24 hours a day and never sleep.)

Then David eats breakfast. His hunger level goes way down, so his grouchiness disappears, and Karla feels more positive toward him. A similar sequence occurs in connection with each meal.

A two-day graph might look something like this, where the jumps represent David's mealtimes:

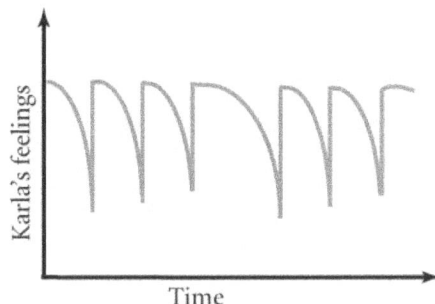

The details of this graph are not important. What is important is the relationship by which each variable depends on another.

Introducing Variables and Function Names

Ask students, **What are the key elements involved in the relationships in this problem?** Have them introduce a variable to describe each element; for example:
- t represents time.
- h represents David's hunger level.
- g represents David's amount of grouchiness.
- p represents the extent of Karla's positive feelings toward David.

Then ask, **Which variable is a function of which other variable?** Students should note three things:
- h is a function of t.
- g is a function of h.
- p is a function of g.

Introduce letter names for each of these functions, perhaps using capital letters. For example:
- $h = U(t)$
- $g = V(h)$
- $p = W(g)$

Bring out that the function students graphed is a combination of these three functions. Then show that they can write

$$p = W(V(U(t)))$$

by starting with $p = W(g)$, replacing g with $V(h)$ to get $p = W(V(h))$, and then replacing h with $U(t)$ to get $p = W(V(U(t)))$.

Composition and Composition Notation

Help students see that overall, p depends on t. If this connection is expressed by the equation $p = F(t)$, the function F represents some sort of combination of the three functions U, V, and W.

Introduce the term **composition of functions** for this method of combining functions. Then sketch a function machine like this one to show how the three functions are combined:

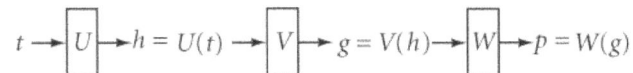

$$t \longrightarrow \boxed{U} \longrightarrow h = U(t) \longrightarrow \boxed{V} \longrightarrow g = V(h) \longrightarrow \boxed{W} \longrightarrow p = W(g)$$

Also introduce the notation

$$W \circ V \circ U$$

for the function obtained by combining U, V, and W in this way. In other words, we can write $p = (W \circ V \circ U)(t)$ and $F = W \circ V \circ U$.

Tell students that an expression like $W \circ V \circ U$ can be read either as "W of V of U" or as "W composition V composition U." Also explain that any function created by the composition of two or more functions is called a *composite function*.

Point out that in the notation $W \circ V \circ U$, the function farthest to the right is done first, and we work from right to left. So, we start from t, apply U to that to get h, then apply V to get g, and finally apply W to get p. (*Order Among the Functions* explores the noncommutativity of composition.)

Key Questions

What are the key elements involved in the relationships in this problem? Which variable is a function of which other variable?

The Composition of Functions

Intent

Students examine how composition is reflected in graphs and tables.

Mathematics

Two new situations introduce students to how composition of functions affects graphs and tables.

Progression

For each of two problem situations, students are given a graph or table of a function and are asked to create a graph or table of another function that is a function of the given function. The follow-up discussion introduces names for the functions to make the role of composition explicit and reviews of the use of composition notation.

Approximate Time

25 to 30 minutes for activity (at home or in class)
15 to 20 minutes for discussion

Classroom Organization

Individuals or small groups, followed by whole-class discussion

Doing the Activity

The activity requires little or no introduction.

Discussing and Debriefing the Activity

The activity calls for numeric calculations of various kinds. The key is getting students to identify the specific functions involved and to recognize the role of composition in the situations.

Question 1

Students will probably do a week-by-week computation to get a graph of Maria's savings each week. You can have volunteers give each numeric result.

Then ask the class, **What are the key elements in the problem? How can you represent their relationships using variables and functions?** We will use w to represent the week number, e to represent Maria's earnings in a given week, and s to represent her savings in a given week. Students should see that e is a function of w and that s is a function of e.

Encourage students to identify and label these functions in some way, such as $e = F(w)$ and $s = G(e)$. Then ask, **How can you express the overall situation using composition?** As needed, review the composition notation that $s = (G \circ F)(w)$, which is equivalent to $s = G(F(w))$.

Also ask, **How are each of the two basic functions, F and G, presented in the problem?** Here, F is presented by means of the graph, and G is presented in verbal terms ("Maria gives \$50 of her earnings to her mother and saves half of the rest.")

How can you express G in algebraic terms? Students might write $G(e) = \frac{1}{2}(e - 50)$. **How can you express Maria's savings each week in terms of these symbols?** For example, they can represent Maria's earnings in week 2 as $F(2)$ and her savings for that week as $G(F(2))$. It appears from the graph that she earned \$80 in the second week, so $F(2) = 80$, and $G(80) = \frac{1}{2}(80 - 50)$, which comes out to \$15. In other words, $G(F(2)) = 15$.

Getting One Graph from Another

You might ask how students could get one graph directly from the other, using the equation $G(e) = \frac{1}{2}(e - 50)$ and the ideas in *The Arithmetic of Graphs*. They may see that they can first move each point of the original graph down 50 units (dollars) and then move each result halfway to the x-axis. It may be instructive for them to see the two graphs on the same set of axes, like this:

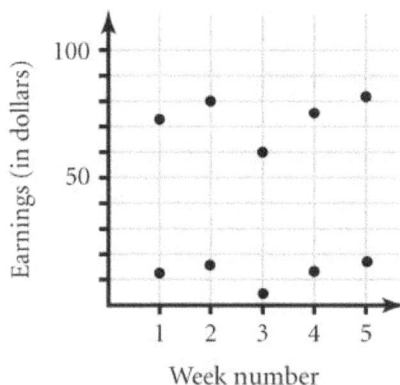

Question 2

Begin by having students share and explain their numeric results, and then discuss the key elements and functions involved. We will use m to represent the month (which is simply the name of the month, not a number), s to represent the number of subscriptions Mario sells in a given month, and e to represent the amount he earns in a given month.

Ask, **Which variable is a function of which other variable?** Students should see that e is a function of s and that s is a function of m. Have them identify and label these functions in some way, such as $s = H(m)$ for the number of subscriptions sold as a function of the month and $e = K(s)$ for Mario's earnings as a function of the number of subscriptions sold. Also have the class express the situation in terms of composition; for example, $e = K(H(m))$ or $e = (K \cdot H)(m)$.

You might point out that H is presented explicitly as a table, while K needs to be developed from the information in the first table in the problem.

The Function K

Ask students to develop an explicit table and graph for K, as it's useful to have them see the function in both ways. Because K is a discrete function, its graph will consist of a set of individual points, as shown here:

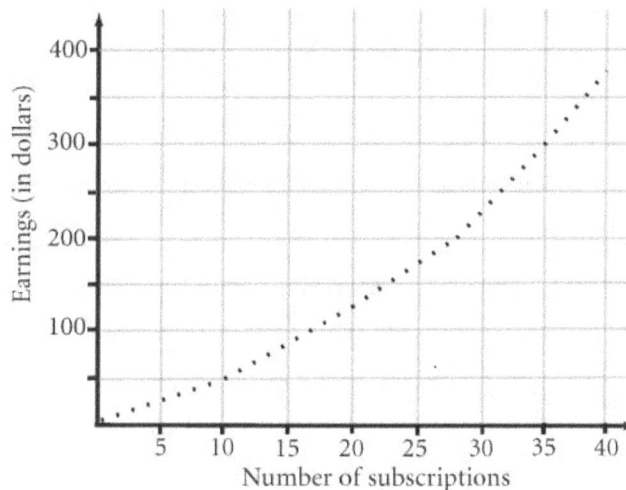

Although these points may appear to be part of a smooth curve, they actually come from four distinct line segments. Students may, in fact, sketch the graph explicitly as a connected series of line segments with increasing slope, like this:

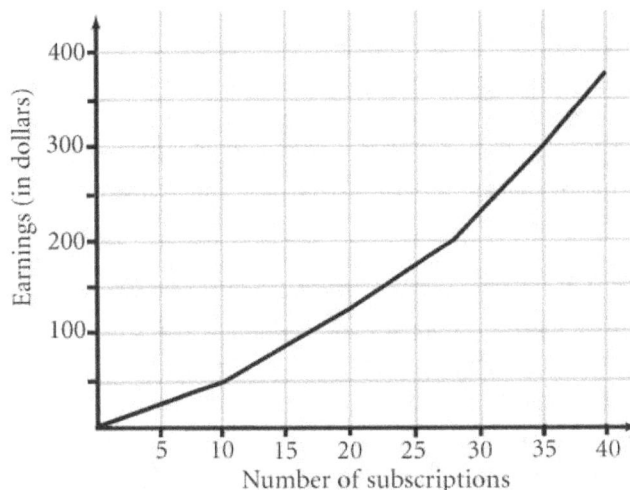

In having students develop a table for *K*, you may want to focus on those rows used in the problem—that is, that correspond to the sales numbers given in Question 2b.

For example, Mario sells 7 subscriptions in September and earns $5 for each of them for a total of $35. In October, he sells 15 subscriptions, so his earnings for that month are $10 \cdot \$5 + 5 \cdot \$7.50 = \$87.50$. Thus, the In-Out table for *K* should include these rows:

s	*K(s)*
7	35
15	87.50

Have students combine this information about *K* with information about *H* and express the results symbolically using composition. For instance, *H*(September) = 7 and *K*(7) = $35, so (*K·H*)(September) = $35. Similarly, *H*(October) = 15 and *K*(15) = $87.50, so (*K·H*)(October) = $87.50.

Mario's Total

Don't forget to deal with the issue posed in Question 2c. By adding the values of (*K·H*)(*m*) for all the months, students should see that Mario does get to go on his trip.

Key Questions

What are the key elements in the problem? How can you represent their relationships using variables and functions?
How can you express the overall situation using composition?
How are each of the two basic functions, *F* and *G*, presented in the problem?
How can you express *G* in algebraic terms?
How can you express Maria's savings each week in terms of the symbols?
Which variable is a function of which other variable?

The Cost of Pollution

Intent

Students work with another situation involving composition.

Mathematics

This activity provides another example of composition of functions.

Progression

Students investigate a situation involving two linear functions, one of which is a function of the other.

Approximate Time

55 to 60 minutes

Classroom Organization

Small groups, followed by whole-class discussion

Doing the Activity

You may want to help students get started by developing the diagram for Question 1 as a class. For instance, it might look like this:

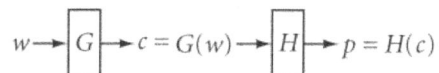

$$w \longrightarrow \boxed{G} \longrightarrow c = G(w) \longrightarrow \boxed{H} \longrightarrow p = H(c)$$

Discussing and Debriefing the Activity

Ask volunteers to present Question 1 and the two parts of Question 2. For the first part of Question 2, all that's needed is to replace c with $50 - 5w$ in the equation $p = 24 - 0.4c$. This gives $p = 24 - 0.4(50 - 5w)$. Have the presenter simplify this to get $p = 4 + 2w$.

It may seem strange to students that the price of catfish dinners goes up when the lake is more polluted. Who would pay more for toxic fish? One potential explanation is that nobody in the fishing industry knows why there are fewer catfish available and that the restaurant doesn't realize that the catfish may not be healthy to eat. Under these circumstances, the decreasing supply of catfish naturally results in an increase in their price.

For the second part of Question 2, the presenter should write p symbolically in terms of w as $p = H(G(w))$ or $p = (H \cdot G)(w)$.

Questions 3 to 5

Some students may have approached Question 3 by first finding the value of c [computing $G(0) = 50$] and substituting to get $H(50) = 4$. Others may have used the equation $p = 4 + 2w$ (found in Question 2), replacing w with 0 directly to get $p = 4$. Have students identify the number 4 here as the price (in dollars) of a dinner.

Similarly, for Question 4, some students may have used c as an intermediate variable, finding that a cost of $12 means 30 catfish per acre and then noting that this means 4 gallons of waste dumped per day. Others may have used the composition equation and solved the equation $12 = 4 + 2w$ to get $w = 4$. Clarify that this 4 represents the amount of waste (in gallons) the company is dumping.

Explore both approaches for Questions 3 and 4 to strengthen students' understanding of the meaning of composition.

For Question 5, students should be able to use the equation $c = 50 - 5w$ to figure out that to get $c = 0$, $w = 10$.

Question 6

Decide whether to have students share their own situations involving composite functions. One possibility is to have them switch problems with another group and discuss the other group's problems.

Order Among the Functions

Intent

Students explore the commutativity of composition of functions.

Mathematics

Through their work, students will recognize that composition of functions is not commutative.

Progression

Students create equations for the composition of each of two functions in both possible orders. They will observe that the results are not equivalent and, therefore, composition is not commutative. For each of the given functions, they then create a function whose composition with the given function *is* commutative.

Approximate Time

30 minutes for activity (at home or in class)
15 to 20 minutes for discussion

Classroom Organization

Individuals, followed by whole-class discussion

Doing the Activity

This activity requires no introduction.

Discussing and Debriefing the Activity

Question 1

Have volunteers describe how they found $f \cdot g$ and $g \cdot f$. They might begin with the appropriate function machine. For instance, the function machine for $f \cdot g$ looks like this:

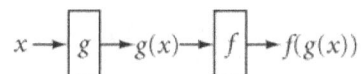

$$x \rightarrow \boxed{g} \rightarrow g(x) \rightarrow \boxed{f} \rightarrow f(g(x))$$

By direct computation, students should see that $(f \cdot g)(x) = 7x + 3$ and $(g \cdot f)(x) = 7(x + 3)$. Presumably, they will recognize that $7x + 3$ and $7(x + 3)$ are not equivalent expressions. You might emphasize this by having them compute both composite functions for a specific value of *x,* such as *x* = 1, and note that the outputs are different.

Summarize Question 1 by asking, **Is composition commutative?** You might use this occasion to review the concept of commutativity more generally by looking at other operations, both commutative and noncommutative, with which students are familiar. In particular, bring up the example of matrix multiplication, which is another familiar noncommutative operation.

Question 2

Ask if anyone had examples for either part a or part b. Students will likely find that functions of the form $h(x) = x + c$ fit the condition in part a and that functions of the form $k(x) = cx$ fit the condition in part b. In particular, they might see that *f* itself works in part a and that *g* itself works in part b.

If no one came up with any examples, you might focus on part a and ask, **What can be done after adding 3 to a number that would lead to the same overall result as doing it before adding 3 to the number?** Students will probably see, for instance, that the "add 5" function will work, because adding 3 and then adding 5 to a number gives the same result as adding 5 and then adding 3. Use a similar approach, if needed, for part b.

Tell students that although composition is not commutative, it's helpful to have a phrase to describe pairs of functions for which the order *does not* matter. If two functions f_1 and f_2 have the property that $f_1 \cdot f_2 = f_2 \cdot f_1$, we say these two functions *commute* with each other.

Ask, **How can you state Question 2a using this language?** Students should say that it asks for a function *h* that commutes with *f.*

A Special Example: The Identity Function

One specific example to elicit is the case of the identity function. To do this, you might ask, **Are there any functions that commute with both *f* and *g*—that is, functions that fit the conditions for both Questions 2a and 2b?**

If necessary, mention that an important—though seemingly trivial—function is the function whose output is always the same as its input. Although there is no standard notation for this function, we will represent it by the letter *I.* Thus, the function *I* is defined by the equation $I(x) = x$.

Tell students that *I* is the **identity function,** sometimes referred to informally as the "do-nothing" function. You can give informal meaning to the term *identity function* by pointing out that the output is "identical" to the input.

If students saw earlier that "addition" functions commute with *f,* they should see now that the identity function can be thought of as "adding 0," so it commutes with *f.* Similarly, if they saw that "multiplication" functions commute with *g,* they can view the identity function as "multiplying by 1," so it commutes with *g.*

Key Questions

Is composition commutative?
What can be done after adding 3 to a number that would lead to the same overall result as doing it before adding 3 to the number?
How can you state Question 2a using this language?
Are there are any functions that commute with both *f* and *g*?

Cozying Up to Composition

Intent

Students continue to work with the composition of functions.

Mathematics

Part I focuses on the mechanics of composition. Part II looks at a familiar situation that can be viewed in terms of composition and is largely preparatory for *Taking Functions Apart.* In that activity, students will look more fully at the process of expressing complex functions as the composition of simpler ones.

Progression

In Part I, students evaluate various compositions of four given functions for specific values and then find equations for several composite functions. Part II returns to a familiar problem to illustrate that students have used the concept of composition before, although without the vocabulary or notation.

Approximate Time

30 minutes for activity (at home or in class)
15 minutes for discussion

Classroom Organization

Individuals, followed by whole-class discussion

Doing the Activity

This activity requires no introduction.

Discussing and Debriefing the Activity

For Part I, the results should be fairly straightforward, but clarify any misconceptions. You might use students' work in Questions 1a and 1b to help the class with Questions 2a and 2b.

Here are the answers for Part I:
- Question 1a: 99
- Question 1b: 368
- Question 1c: 256
- Question 1d: −5

- Question 2a: $(g \cdot f)(x) = 6x^2 + 3$
- Question 2b: $(f \cdot g)(x) = 12x^2 - 84x + 152$
- Question 2c: $(f \cdot k)(x) = 3 \sin^2 x + 5$
- Question 2d: $(h \cdot g)(x) = 2^{2x-7}$
- Question 2e: $(f \cdot f)(x) = 27x^4 + 90x^2 + 80$
- Question 2f: $(g \cdot g \cdot g)(x) = 8x - 49$

For Question 3, students should recognize that the area can be described by the equation $A(t) = \pi(70 + 6t)^2$, where t is the number of hours since Lindsay first saw the oil slick.

The discussion of Question 4 is important preparation for *Taking Functions Apart.* If students had trouble, give them a specific value for t and ask how they would find the area. **What steps would you use to find the area for $t = 9$?** For $t = 9$, they would probably first compute the radius (that is, find the value of $70 + 6 \cdot 9$) and substitute the result, 124, into the formula for the area of a circle.

Point out that each of these steps is a function, so students can define a function g by $g(t) = 70 + 6t$ and a second function h by $h(r) = \pi r^2$. Help them to see that using these definitions, they get $(h \cdot g)(t) = A(t)$.

Key Question

What steps would you use to find the area for $t = 9$?

Supplemental Activity

Over, and Over, and Over, and . . . **(extension)** focuses on the process of composing a function with itself (such as in Questions 2e and 2f), or *iteration*.

Taking Functions Apart

Intent

Students decompose functions.

Mathematics

This activity continues the work from Part II of *Cozying Up to Composition*. The process of breaking down a function is used to apply rules for differentiation and integration in calculus.

Progression

Students write each of six functions as the composition of two or more other functions.

Approximate Time

20 to 25 minutes for activity (at home or in class)
10 minutes for discussion

Classroom Organization

Small groups or individuals, followed by whole-class discussion

Doing the Activity

This activity requires no introduction.

Discussing and Debriefing the Activity

Have students offer solutions to each problem, with other students suggesting alternative solutions. If no one offers a solution in which the given function is written as the composition of more than two functions, you might mention one so students see this option.

For instance, in Question 3, one solution is to define functions such as $g(x) = 3x^2 - 6$ and $h(w) = w^5$, so the given function is $h \cdot g$. (We are using an intermediate variable to clarify the two steps.) But it would be illuminating for students to see that they can decompose g by defining $H(x) = x^2$ and $K(x) = 3x - 6$, so $g = K \cdot H$ (and the original function is $h \cdot K \cdot H$). In fact, even K can be decomposed into two simpler functions.

Here are possible answers for the other questions. In each case, the original function is equal to the composite $h = f \cdot g$.

- Question 1: $g(x) = x^2$, $f(x) = 3y$
- Question 2: $g(x) = \sin x$, $f(x) = \dfrac{1}{y}$
- Question 4: $g(x) = x^2 + 2x - 4$, $f(x) = \sqrt{y}$
- Question 5: $g(x) = x^2 + 1$, $f(x) = \ln y$
- Question 6: $g(x) = x + 2$, $f(x) = 3^y + 7$

Fish, Ladders, and Bacteria

Intent

Students find the inverse of several functions.

Mathematics

This activity provides the context for introducing the general concept of inverse functions. Students see that not every function has an inverse. They also learn that the domain of a function is equal to the range of its inverse function, and conversely the range of a function is equal to the domain of its inverse.

Progression

Each of the three problems in this activity gives an equation for one variable in terms of a second and asks students to find a general expression for the second variable in terms of the first. The subsequent discussion introduces the definition and notation of an inverse function, as well as the concepts of domain and range in the context of inverse functions.

Approximate Time

25 to 30 minutes for activity (at home or in class)
25 to 30 minutes for discussion

Classroom Organization

Individuals or small groups, followed by whole-class discussion

Doing the Activity

This activity requires no introduction.

Discussing and Debriefing the Activity

Focus the discussion on developing the general expressions asked for in part b of each question. Have students use the specific examples from part a to explain how they found the general expressions.

In Question 1, students should have no trouble finding that they need $w = 6$ to get $c = 20$. Clarify the generalization, if necessary, by doing some other numeric examples. Be sure students see how to get the general expression $\dfrac{50-c}{5}$ as the amount of waste that will yield c catfish per acre.

For Question 2, you may want to point out that the general expression $\sin^{-1}\left(\dfrac{h}{12}\right)$ doesn't make sense if h is greater than 12. This is logical, because otherwise it would mean that the top of the 12-foot ladder was more than 12 feet off the ground.

In the context of Question 2, h must be positive and θ must be acute, so we don't have to worry about the fact that there are many angles with the same sine. (The answer to Question 2a is 66°.)

For Question 3b, review ideas about logarithms as needed to get the general expression $\log_2\left(\dfrac{b}{50}\right)$ for t. (The answer to Question 3a is 4.3 hours.)

Inverse Functions

Ask, **What do these three problems have in common?** Students were asked to think about this in the introduction to the activity. They will probably say something like, "They required you to turn the problem around" or "You had to switch which variable was in terms of the other one."

Explain that these three problems illustrate one more way of making new functions from old ones. This new method is called finding the **inverse of a function.**

Introduce the notation for an inverse function. For example, introduce the letter G for the function expressing c, the number of catfish per acre, in terms of w, the amount of waste dumped per day. You might start by writing this "generically" as the equation $c = G(w)$ and then ask, **What is an explicit equation for G in terms of w?** Namely, $G(w) = 50 - 5w$.

Then point out that in Question 1, students, in essence, found a function that expresses w in terms of c. Introduce the notation G^{-1} for this new function, and ask for an explicit equation $G^{-1}(c)$. Students simply need to use their answer to Question 1, as G^{-1} is defined by the equation $G^{-1}(c) = \dfrac{50-c}{5}$.

Tell students that the inverse of a function can be thought of intuitively as "undoing" what the original function does. Illustrate by starting with a specific value for w. For instance, using $w = 4$, have students first find $G(4)$ using the expression

$50 - 5 \cdot 4$, which equals 30, and then find $G^{-1}(30)$, using the expression $\dfrac{50 - 30}{5}$, which equals 4. Emphasize that they are back to their original value. That is, $G^{-1}(G(4)) = 4$.

Inverse Functions and Question 2

Introduce the letter K to represent the function given in Question 2—that is, define K by the equation $K(\theta) = 12 \sin \theta$. Then ask, **What is an equation for K^{-1}?** Students will probably use the variable h as the input for K^{-1} and write

$$k^{-1}(h) = \sin^{-1}\left(\frac{h}{12}\right).$$

Now illustrate that K^{-1} "undoes" K. For instance, have students find $K(60°)$, which is approximately 10.4, and then find $K^{-1}(10.4)$. They should see that this gives 60°. [If they rounded $K(60°)$, they may not get exactly 60° when they apply K^{-1}.]

Have the class go through the same process for an angle in the second quadrant, such as 130°. When students see they do not get back to 130°, ask, **Why don't you get back to where you started if you use 130°?** They will probably recognize that the value they get, 50°, is the reference angle for 130°. Bring out that $K(50°)$ and $K(130°)$ are both equal to roughly 9.2, and $K^{-1}(9.2)$ cannot be both 50° and 130°.

Explain that because of this dilemma, there is no true inverse for the sine function. You might also mention that the function represented as $\sin^{-1}$ is technically only the inverse of *part* of the sine function.

Domain and Range for Functions and Their Inverses

This is a good opportunity to review the terminology of *domain* and *range* (see the discussion introducing *Brake!*) and to discuss how these two sets relate to functions and their inverses.

You might start with the function G from Question 1. The domain for G is the set of possible amounts of toxic waste per day, expressed in gallons. The range for G is the set of possibilities for the number of catfish per acre. You might introduce a schematic diagram like this:

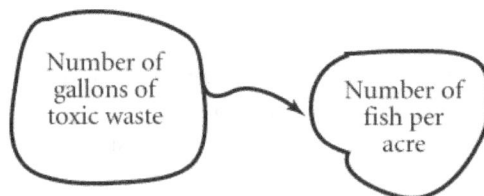

Number of gallons of toxic waste → Number of fish per acre

Then ask, **What are the domain and range for G^{-1}?** Students should see that the roles are reversed. That is, the domain for G^{-1} is the same as the range for G, and the range for G^{-1} is the same as the domain for G. Or, we could say that the output for G becomes the input for G^{-1}, and the input for G becomes the output for G^{-1}.

Domain and Range in Question 3

The focus here should be on inverse functions, so if the example of exponential and logarithmic functions creates difficulties, you may want to use a different example, such as squaring and taking a square root.

Introduce the letter H to represent the function in Question 3, namely, $H(t) = 50 \cdot 2^t$. Tell students to consider this function independently of the context of the problem, and ask, **What is the domain of the function defined by the equation $H(t) = 50 \cdot 2^t$?** They should see that t can be any value.

Then ask about the range of H. You may need to help students understand that $H(t)$ must be positive but that *any* positive output is possible. Also, outputs less than 50 require negative inputs for t.

Then have the class consider the inverse function H^{-1}. First, have students get an explicit equation for H^{-1}. They should see that this is a repetition of their work in Question 3b and that H^{-1} is defined by the equation $H^{-1}(b) = \log_2\left(\dfrac{b}{50}\right)$.

Then ask, **What are the domain and range for H^{-1}?** Help students to see that the expression $\log_2\left(\dfrac{b}{50}\right)$ is defined only for positive values of b, so the domain of H^{-1} is the set of positive real numbers. Bring out that the domain of H^{-1} is equal to the range of H. Similarly, the range of H^{-1} is the set of all real numbers, which is equal to the domain of H.

You may want to point out that the domain and range for a function in a specific context may be different from the domain and range when the equation defining the function is used abstractly. For example, in Question 3, H is defined by the equation $H(t) = 50 \cdot 2^t$. Although this equation defines a function for all real numbers t, the context of the problem suggests using only positive values for t. In fact, the equation may fit the situation only for "small" values of t.

Key Questions

What do these three problems have in common?
What is an explicit equation for G in terms of w?
What's an equation for K^{-1}?
Why don't you get back to where you started if you use 130°?

What are the domain and range for G^{-1}?

What is the domain of the function defined by the equation $H(t) = 50 \cdot 2^t$?

What are the domain and range for H^{-1}?

Functions in Verse

Intent

Students investigate the relationships between a function and its inverse in terms of tables and graphs.

Mathematics

Students explore the relationships between the tables of a function and its inverse and between the graphs of a function and its inverse. The follow-up discussion defines the identity function and the inverse function.

Progression

After exploring the tables for three functions and their inverses, students make a statement of the general relationship between the table of a function and the table of its inverse. They then follow a similar procedure for the graphs of functions and their inverses. The subsequent discussion brings out that the table for an inverse function is obtained by switching the two columns of the table for the original function, and the graph of an inverse function is the reflection of the graph of the original function across the line $y = x$. After a brief review of identity and inverse elements, the discussion defines the identity function and inverse function as the identity and inverse, respectively, for the operation of composition.

Approximate Time

50 minutes

Classroom Organization

Small groups, followed by whole-class discussion

Doing the Activity

As groups finish the activity, ask them to prepare presentations on various parts of it for discussion.

Discussing and Debriefing the Activity

Have students from different groups make presentations for each of Questions 1 to 3. They should report that the pairs of numbers in the table for an inverse function are obtained from the original function merely by reversing the order of the numbers. For example, in Question 3, the pair (3, 7) in the table for h leads to the pair (7, 3) in the table for h^{-1}; that is, $h^{-1}(7) = 3$.

For Question 4, students might explain the general principle like this: "An ordered pair in a function table will appear in reverse order in the table for the inverse function, because the inverse function takes $f(x)$ back to x."

For Question 5, students should recognize that the graph for each inverse function is the reflection of the function across the line $y = x$. They may express this in terms of "switching coordinates" rather than in clear geometric terms. To help clarify the geometry, you might ask, **How are the points of the inverse graph related geometrically to the points of the original graph?** Try to elicit the word **reflection** in the description.

Identity and Inverse Functions

Ask students, **In what other contexts have you used the word *inverse*?** They might think of multiplicative inverses—that is, reciprocals of numbers—or inverses of matrices, as well as inverse trigonometric functions. Help them also recall that the term **inverse** is used for situations in which two numbers (or other objects) are combined to get the **identity** element for a given operation. As needed, review the definition of *identity element* as well.

Keep the focus on simple examples and ordinary (number) multiplication. Addition of numbers and operations on matrices are explored in *An Inventory of Inverses*.

For instance, ask, **What is the identity element for multiplication?** Students should recognize that the answer is 1, because $1 \cdot x = x \cdot 1 = x$, for any number x.

What is the inverse for 5 for the operation of multiplication? Students should say that the multiplicative inverse of 5 is $\frac{1}{5}$, because $5 \cdot \frac{1}{5} = \frac{1}{5} \cdot 5 = 1$.

The Identity Function

Once the general concepts of *identity* and *inverse* seem reasonably clear, return to the subject of functions. Ask, **What function would be the identity element for the operation of composition?**

If necessary, ask, **What does it mean for a function—call it *g* for the moment—to be the identity element for composition?** Help students see that they want $g \cdot f$ to be the same function as f itself (no matter what f is). In other words, "doing f" and then "doing g" should be the same as simply "doing f." This should remind students of the "do-nothing" function introduced in the discussion of *Order Among the Functions*.

Remind students that the "do-nothing" function is generally called the *identity function* and represented by the letter I. Explain that the formal reason for the name *identity function* is that this function is the identity element for the operation of composition.

Point out that as with other operations, the identity for the operation of composition has to work "on both sides." In other words, both $f \cdot I$ and $I \cdot f$ must be equal to f. The identity function fits both conditions.

Acknowledge that there are other operations on functions (as students saw in the activities in *Back to Arithmetic*) and that these operations may have different identity elements. Tell students that the term *identity function* is usually reserved specifically for the identity element for the operation of composition.

With I established as the identity element for composition, ask, **What equation should the inverse of a function *f* satisfy?** It may help to use a specific letter—say, g—to represent the inverse. Bring out that for g to be the inverse of f, we must get the identity when g is "combined" with f (using composition). In other words, $g \cdot f$ must be equal to I. Point out that because I is the "do-nothing" function, this is consistent with the earlier, intuitive idea that the inverse of a function must "undo" that function.

Use examples to illustrate this connection. For instance, you might use function h from Question 1 to illustrate, using tables, how the composition of a function and its inverse give the identity.

Key Questions

How are the points of the inverse graph related geometrically to the points of the original graph?
In what other contexts have you used the word *inverse*?
What is the identity element for multiplication?
What is the inverse for 5 for the operation of multiplication?
What function would be the identity element for the operation of composition?
What does it mean for a function to be the identity element for composition?
What equation should the inverse of a function *f* satisfy?

Linear Functions in Verse

Intent

Students examine the inverses of linear functions.

Mathematics

The activity *Functions in Verse* focused on tables and graphs. *Linear Functions in Verse* begins by reminding students that not every function has an inverse and that some inverses cannot be represented algebraically. It then focuses on the algebra of inverse functions, using the special case of linear functions.

Progression

Given a linear function, students write an equation for the inverse function and then check the inverse function using a table. They also find a general expression for the inverse of a linear function.

Approximate Time

25 minutes for activity (at home or in class)
10 to 15 minutes for discussion

Classroom Organization

Individuals, followed by whole-class discussion

Doing the Activity

This activity requires little or no introduction.

Discussing and Debriefing the Activity

You may want to give students time to discuss the activity in groups and then have a student report on Question 1.

The inverse of *f* is given by the equation $f^{-1}(w) = \frac{1}{3}(w - 2)$. You might check

whether anyone made the common mistake of writing $f^{-1}(w) = \frac{1}{3}w - 2$. Students

can use their work from part b to verify the correct answer.

Ask the class, **Why does the equation** $f^{-1}(w) = \frac{1}{3}(w-2)$ **make intuitive sense?**

Students might find it useful to think of *f* itself as a two-step function, perhaps using a function machine like this one:

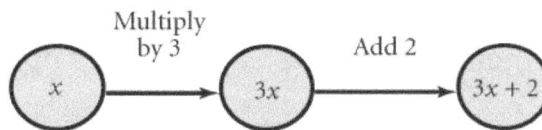

Thus, *f* goes in two steps from the first circle to the last. Help students see that to undo this process, they need to undo the second step of the process before they undo the first step. That is, they must first subtract 2 and then divide by 3.

You might want to use the example of putting on socks and then shoes to bring out the need for undoing the second step first. A person wearing shoes and socks must take the shoes off first, because they were put on second.

Using the variable *w* for the input of the inverse function, students can see that *w* corresponds to 3*x* + 2, so the value 3*x* (in the middle circle) corresponds to *w* − 2.

If students had trouble with Question 1, give them a few minutes to confer in groups on Question 2, and then have another student report. The class should see that f^{-1} is defined by the equation $f^{-1}(w) = \frac{1}{a}\left(w-b\right)$.

Key Question

Why does the equation $f^{-1}(w) = \frac{1}{3}(w-2)$ **make intuitive sense?**

Supplemental Activity

Its Own Inverse **(extension)** asks students to find functions that are their own inverses.

An Inventory of Inverses

Intent

Students find identity elements and inverses for various operations.

Mathematics

This activity continues students' work with identity elements and inverses. Students find identity elements for several operations, including addition and multiplication of matrices. They also consider the "two-sided" nature of the relationship between a function and its inverse.

Progression

The teacher introduces this activity with a brief review of the addition and multiplication of matrices. Students then find identity elements for a few given operations. Next, given a linear function and its inverse, they demonstrate that the inverse is two-sided. Finally, they consider whether an inverse will always exist for each operation addressed in the first part of the activity.

Approximate Time

10 minutes for introduction
30 minutes for activity (at home or in class)
15 minutes for discussion

Classroom Organization

Individuals, followed by whole-class discussion

Doing the Activity

This activity on identity and inverse elements uses matrix algebra as a source of examples, so you may want to briefly review matrix operations. In particular, remind students that they add "like" matrices (matrices with the same dimensions) by adding the corresponding entries, and review the definition of matrix multiplication.

Discussing and Debriefing the Activity

Ask for volunteers to report on the several parts of Questions 1, 2, and 3.

Question 1

Parts b and c provide an opportunity to review ideas about matrices.

In part d, students will have to think carefully about the meaning of *identity element.* Be sure the class sees why "the tallest person in the world" is an identity element for this operation. (If there is a tie for this title, then none of the contenders is an identity element, because an identity element must be two-sided. If R and S are tied for tallest, then R * S = R and S * R = S, according to how the operation is defined for ties. This means neither R nor S is the identity element. The discussion of part d assumes there is a single tallest person.)

Inverses Are Two-Sided

One important aspect of Question 2 is the fact that inverses must be "two-sided." Although this is mentioned in the activity (and may have been discussed briefly with *Functions in Verse*), students will likely have no previous experience with "one-sided" inverses—that is, objects that work as inverses on only one side of the operation symbol.

Discuss this idea briefly before looking at Question 2. If needed, review first that identity elements, as well, must work on both sides. For instance, we have not only $1 \cdot x = x$ but also $x \cdot 1 = x$. In particular, go over this principle for the identity function: for any function *f,* we have not only $I \cdot f = f$ but also $f \cdot I = f$.

Then review the two-sided nature of inverses for one or two familiar examples, such as $\frac{1}{5} \cdot 5 = 1$ and $5 \cdot \frac{1}{5} = 1$, or $5 + (-5) = 0$ and $(-5) + 5 = 0$. Tell students that, strictly speaking, the inverse of a function (for composition) also has to work on both sides.

Question 2

Have students present the parts of Question 2. For parts a and b, they need only go through the computations. For instance, in part a, they should explain that $(f \cdot g)(x)$ means $f\left(\frac{1}{3}(x-2)\right)$, which in turn means $3 \cdot \left[\frac{1}{3}(x-2)\right] + 2$. They then need to show that this expression simplifies to x.

For part c, they should see that with k defined by the equation $k(x) = 4x^3 - 5$, the inverse for k is the function h defined by the equation $h(x) = \sqrt[3]{\frac{x+5}{4}}$. Have them confirm that h and k are inverses.

You can also use this example as an opportunity to review the principle that to undo a sequence of steps, you undo the individual steps in the opposite order from which they were originally done. In the case of part c, the function k can be seen as a sequence of three steps: Take the cube, multiply by 4, and subtract 5. The inverse h also consists of three steps: Add 5, divide by 4, and take the cube root.

A One-Sided Inverse

Ask students what they would expect as the inverse for the function f defined by the equation $f(x) = x^2$. **What would you expect as the inverse for the squaring function?** They will doubtless see that the natural candidate is the function g defined by $g(z) = \sqrt{z}$.

Ask them to check whether this really works. As needed, help them see the difficulties. The main problem is that the composite function $g \cdot f$ is not the identity function—for example, $(g \cdot f)(-2) \neq -2$. (It is true that $f \cdot g = I$.)

Point out that this dilemma can be rectified by restricting the domain of f to be just the nonnegative numbers. (Of course, g itself is already restricted in this way, unless students consider imaginary numbers.) Help students see that if the domain of f is restricted, then f and g are inverses of each other in the two-sided sense.

You might ask students to consider other examples of functions with similar limitations, such as the inverse trigonometric functions.

Question 3

Parts a to c should be fairly routine, although part c may require some review of matrices.

For part d, it turns out that only the identity element (the tallest person) has an inverse. (We are assuming that there is a unique tallest person. Otherwise, there is no identity element.)

We will call the identity element T. To help students see that only T has an inverse, you may want to have them explicitly write down the equation that an inverse needs to satisfy. That is, for A and B to be inverses means that $A * B = B * A = T$. But $A * B$ is the *shorter* of A and B, so this can't be T unless A and B are both T.

Key Question

What would you expect as the inverse for the squaring function?

Transforming Functions

Intent

In these activities, students examine the formation of new functions by transforming functions.

Mathematics

These activities examine how transforming the algebraic representation of a function affects it table and graph.

Progression

Double Dose of Functions and *Slide That Function* introduce the concept of transformation of a function and explore the effect of the transformation on the graph of the function. *Transforming Graphs, Tables, and Situations* generalizes students' work to arbitrary tables and graphs.

Double Dose of Functions
Slide That Function
Transforming Graphs, Tables, and Situations

Double Dose of Functions

Intent

This activity introduces the transformation of functions.

Mathematics

In this activity, students explore two specific ways to **transform** a function—by doubling the output of the function and then by doubling the input of the function—and examine the effect on the graphs of the functions.

Progression

Students begin to look at how the graph of a function is affected if the function is transformed. They discover that doubling the output stretches the graph vertically, while doubling the input squeezes the graph horizontally. In the follow-up discussion, they generalize their findings to multiplying by any factor. The discussion also explores the relationship between doubling and composition with the doubling function.

Approximate Time

25 to 30 minutes for activity (at home or in class)
10 minute for discussion

Classroom Organization

Small groups or individuals, followed by whole-class discussion

Doing the Activity

Tell students they will now look at yet another way to create new functions.

Discussing and Debriefing the Activity

Have a few students report on their investigations, including their examples for Questions 1c and 2c. For both Questions 1 and 2, it's best if students describe in their own words the changes in the graphs that result from the algebraic transformations.

Question 1

Students should see that the graph of the equation $y = 2f(x)$ is twice as high at a given x-value as the graph of $y = f(x)$. They can think of the graph as being stretched in the vertical direction.

Students may see the principle here most clearly if they consider tables for both functions in a given pair. For instance, if they pick $x = 20°$ in Question 1a, they will see that they find the value of the function $y = 2 \sin x$ by simply doubling $\sin 20°$. Thus, the point $(20°, 0.342)$ is on the graph of one function while $(20°, 0.684)$ is on the graph of the other.

Question 2

This question may be a bit more difficult. Starting with the example $y = \sin x$ should be helpful, because the horizontal scale is so important in periodicity. In general, the graph of $y = f(2x)$ can be thought of as being obtained by "squeezing" the graph of $y = f(x)$ horizontally by a factor of 2.

Working with a table may be helpful here as well. You might have students consider what happens for a "generic" function. For example, ask, If (3, 7) is on the graph of $y = f(x)$, what point is on the graph of $y = f(2x)$? It may help to have students write this in function notation as $7 = f(3)$. Then have them find a point on the graph of $y = f(2x)$. They should see that they know only the value of $f(3)$, so they need to make the input, $2x$, equal to 3. That is, they should consider $x = 1.5$ and see that $f(2 \cdot 1.5) = 7$, so $(1.5, 7)$ is on the graph of $y = f(2x)$.

Students may be surprised that multiplying the input by 2 "squeezes" rather than "stretches" the graph. It is a common error to think that if (3, 7) is a point on the graph of $y = f(x)$, the related point on the graph of $y = f(2x)$ should be (6, 7).

Generalizing Beyond Factors of 2

Ask students to generalize their conclusions to the case of factors other than 2, which should be fairly straightforward.

Relation to Composition

Ask students, How can you express the function $y = 2f(x)$ using composition? Help them to see that if they define a "doubling function" d by the equation $d(x) = 2x$, then the function $y = 2f(x)$ is the composite function $d \cdot f$. Then ask, How can you express the function defined by the equation $y = f(2x)$? Elicit the idea that this is the composite function $f \cdot d$. You might also use this discussion to emphasize that the operation of composition is not commutative.

Key Questions

If (3, 7) is on the graph of $y = f(x)$, what point is on the graph of $y = f(2x)$?

How can you express the function $y = 2f(x)$ using composition? How about $y = f(2x)$?

Slide That Function

Intent

Students continue to examine the effect of transformations on the graphs of functions.

Mathematics

This activity is a variation on *Double Dose of Functions.* It focuses on additive rather than multiplicative changes.

Progression

Students investigate the effect on the graph of a function when the function is transformed by adding a fixed value to the output or by adding a fixed value to the input.

Approximate Time

30 minutes for activity (at home or in class)
15 to 20 minutes for discussion

Classroom Organization

Individuals or small groups, followed by whole-class discussion

Doing the Activity

This activity requires little or no introduction.

Discussing and Debriefing the Activity

Let volunteers share some of their examples and their conclusions.

Students may be surprised that adding a positive number to the input moves the graph to the left rather than to the right. Point out the analogy between this situation and their experience with Question 2 of *Double Dose of Functions*. That is, when changes are made to the input variable (either multiplying or adding) before applying the function, the change in the graph is opposite to the corresponding kind of change in the output variable.

Looking at a table may give students more understanding of this apparent reversal. Or you might point out that if the input to the function is changed from x to $x + 2$, then a smaller value of x (not a larger one) is needed to achieve the same output as before.

Transforming Graphs, Tables, and Situations

Intent

Students generalize the work they have been doing on transformations to arbitrary tables and graphs.

Mathematics

Students examine the relationship between the transformation of functions and various representations of those functions.

Progression

Presented first with a graph and then with a table of an unidentified function, students sketch the graphs or create tables for four transformations of the function. The final question asks how a function, which gives the height in feet of a bouncing ball in terms of time in seconds, would have to be transformed to use inches instead of feet or minutes instead of seconds. The discussion again brings out that transformations applied to the input have effects on graphs that may seem the opposite of what one might expect.

Approximate Time

30 minutes for activity (at home or in class)
20 minutes for discussion

Classroom Organization

Individuals, followed by whole-class discussion

Materials

Transparency of *Transforming Graphs, Tables, and Situations* blackline master

Doing the Activity

This activity requires little or no introduction.

Discussing and Debriefing the Activity

You might give students a few minutes in their groups to come to consensus on their answers before beginning the discussion.

Question 1

We suggest that you project the graph in Question 1 and have different students each draw one of the graphs from parts a to d on it.

We provide here the four pairs of graphs, with brief comments on each.

The new graph for part a, for $y = f(x) - 3$, is created by moving the original graph down 3 units.

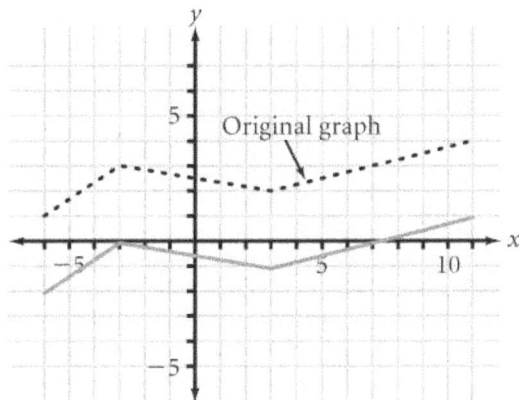

The new graph for part b, for $y = f(x + 2)$, is created by moving the original graph to the left 2 units. Notice that the domain for this function is different from that of the original function.

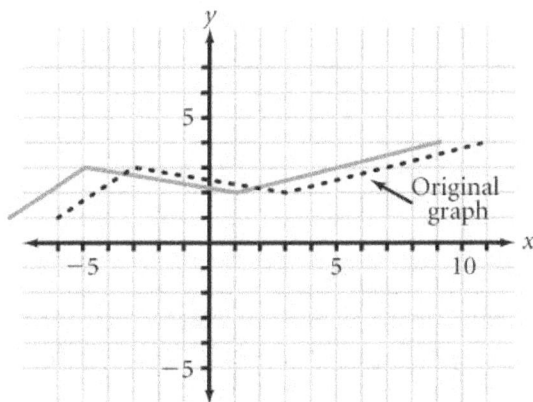

By now, students will probably no longer be surprised that adding 2 to x moves the graph to the left rather than to the right. If they still find this perplexing, a numeric example may be helpful. For instance, the original graph includes the point (3, 2), so $f(3) = 2$. We need to substitute 1 for x in the equation $y = f(x + 2)$ to use the fact that $f(3) = 2$. From the point (3, 2) on the original graph, we get the point (1, 2) on the new graph.

The new graph for part c, for $y = \frac{1}{2}f(x)$, is created by multiplying the y-coordinate for each point by $\frac{1}{2}$.

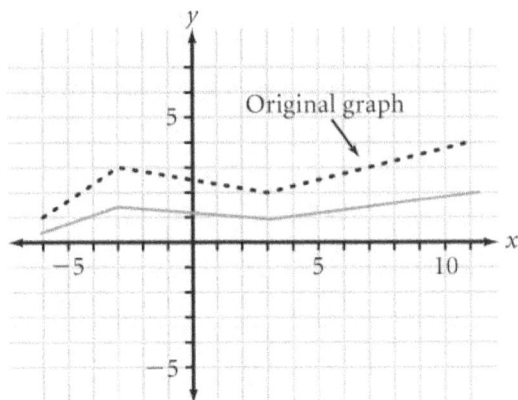

The new graph for part d, for $y = f(2x)$, is created by shrinking the original graph toward the y-axis by a factor of 2. As with part b, this may seem counterintuitive, but students have already seen this phenomenon in *Double Dose of Functions.*

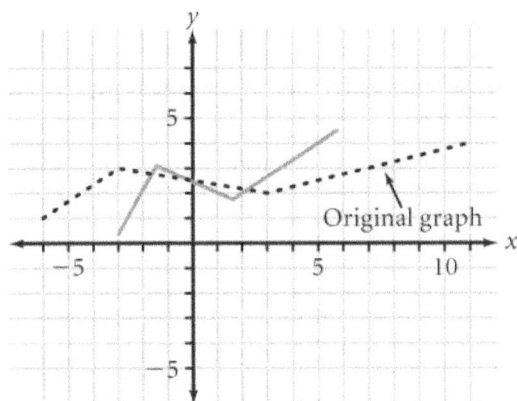

You may want to bring out that as with part b, the domain for the new function is different from the domain for the original function. Students may realize that if the transformation involves changing x *before* applying the function *f* (that is, if the change is to the input of the function), the domain is likely to change.

Question 2

The ideas in Question 2 are similar to those in Question 1, and you may decide there's no need to go over them in detail. The key idea is that the inputs for the tables for parts b and d are different from the inputs for the original table. In both cases, the outputs are the same as in the original table. (In parts a and c, the inputs are the same as in the original table, but the outputs are different.) Here are the most complete tables possible for parts b and d:

x	$g(x-3)$
1	7
2	3
3	2
4	0
5	−3
6	−2
7	0
8	1
9	4

x	$g\left(\frac{1}{2}x\right)$
−4	7
−2	3
0	2
2	0
4	−3
6	−2
8	0
10	1
12	4

Question 3

This question shows the connection between algebraic transformation of functions and changes in ordinary units of measurement. For instance, in part a, students should see that for a given value of x, the ball will bounce 12 times as many inches as it does feet. The key idea is to express this algebraically: $k(x) = 12h(x)$.

Part b is likely to be more difficult, because the result is somewhat counterintuitive (as with all the examples in which the transformation involves changing x *before* applying the original function). A specific example may be helpful. For instance, $j(2)$ represents the height after 2 minutes. This is the same as the height after 120 seconds, so $j(2) = h(120)$. In general, $j(x) = h(60x)$.

Supplemental Activity

A Hyperbolic Approach (extension) explores a situation that leads to the graph of one branch of a hyperbola. Explaining why that situation leads to the hyperbolic graph involves ideas about transformations of functions.

Back to the Beginning

Intent

In these activities, students summarize what they have learned in the unit.

Mathematics

Students apply their new techniques to fitting a function to data and a situation.

Progression

Better Braking is a variation on *Brake!* from the beginning of the unit, allowing students an opportunity to use their greater knowledge of fitting functions and to see another application of combining functions. In *Beginning Portfolio Selection,* students reflect on the connections between the various representations of functions. In *"The World of Functions" Portfolio,* they review the characteristics of the function families and the ways functions can be combined or transformed.

Better Braking
Beginning Portfolio Selection
"The World of Functions" Portfolio

Better Braking

Intent

Students find a function to fit a given set of data.

Mathematics

Students revisit the opening problem, but with a new twist. The data now include reaction time in the stopping distance. Students should realize from the situation that a quadratic function with no constant term will be most appropriate.

Progression

Students are once more trying to fit a function to data for the stopping distance of a car as a function of speed. They will probably use the calculator's quadratic regression feature. The discussion includes other methods of fitting a function to the data, including combining a new function for the reaction-time distance with the function found for the stopping distance in the original activity.

Approximate Time

30 minutes for activity
20 to 40 minutes for discussion

Classroom Organization

Small groups, followed by whole-class discussion

Doing the Activity

Tell students they will now examine a variation on the opening problem of the unit, and let groups begin work.

The key step is realizing that the new data set still seems to fit a quadratic function. Students will probably use quadratic regression to find the best function in the quadratic family. Other approaches are mentioned in the discussion of the activity.

In terms of the situation, one would expect the best fit to be a quadratic function with only quadratic and linear terms. The constant term should still be 0, because the stopping distance is 0 if the car isn't moving. In fact, because the data set represents only approximate values, applying regression yields a quadratic function with a nonzero (but very small) constant term.

Discussing and Debriefing the Activity

Begin the discussion by having two or three students explain their choice of family in looking for a function that fits the data set. They might do this directly on the basis of the data, perhaps noting that the second differences are approximately constant. Another approach is to consider that the rate of deceleration is likely to be constant, which leads to a quadratic function.

Finding a Specific Quadratic Function

Once students decide they are looking for a quadratic function, there are several approaches for finding a specific function that fits the data set well.

One approach is to use the calculator's quadratic regression feature. This should give a function g defined approximately by the equation $g(x) \approx 0.0555x^2 + 1.099x + 0.021$.

Another approach is to compare the table in *Better Braking* with the table in the original problem. The difference between the two tables—that is, the extra distance due to reaction time—is given in this table:

Speed (in miles per hour)	Extra distance due to reaction time (in feet)
20	22.0
25	27.5
30	33.0
35	38.5
40	44.0
45	49.5
50	55.0

Students who do this should see that the extra distance is a linear function of speed. Point out that this makes sense, because the stopping distance for the reaction-time portion should be proportional to the speed.

If we call the new function g and the original function f, then the difference function is $g - f$, and the table shows that $g - f$ is given by the equation $(g - f)(x) = 1.1x$. Because the original function f was represented approximately by the equation $f(x) = 0.0555x^2$, this gives $g(x) = 0.0555x^2 + 1.1x$, which is essentially identical to the function found using regression.

A third method is to assume the equation has the form $f(x) = ax^2 + bx$ (combining the "proportional to the square" portion with the "proportional to x" portion for the reaction time). Students can then pick two of the points, such as the first and last, and set up equations for a and b by substituting the coordinates of these points as values for x and $f(x)$. For example, using (20, 44.2) and (50, 193.8), this gives $400a + 20b = 44.2$ and $2500a + 50b = 193.8$. This gives $a \approx 0.0555$ and $b \approx 1.099$, just like the function found using regression.

Supplemental Activity

"Small World" Again! **(extension or reinforcement)** gives students a chance to apply what they have learned in this unit to data from a unit problem from Year 3.

Beginning Portfolio Selection

Intent

Students begin selecting activities for inclusion in unit portfolio.

Mathematics

The focus of the activity is on the various ways of thinking about functions and the connections among them.

Progression

Students select activities that helped them see connections among the various ways of looking at functions—tables, graphs, equations, and situations—and reflect upon those connections.

Approximate Time

30 minutes for activity (at home or in class)
5 to 10 minutes for discussion

Classroom Organization

Individuals, followed by whole-class discussion

Doing the Activity

This activity requires no introduction.

Discussing and Debriefing the Activity

You might have a couple of volunteers read their descriptions of the activities they chose and the connections they made. You may also want to have some students share their choice of activities from the earlier Year 4 unit or from the previous year that made the same connections.

"The World of Functions" Portfolio

Intent

Students reflect upon the key concepts of the unit as they compile their unit portfolios and write their cover letters.

Mathematics

The instructions for the cover letter ask students to focus on the distinguishing characteristics of each family of functions and on methods of combining and transforming functions.

Progression

Students select activities for inclusion in their unit portfolios and write a cover letter summarizing the unit.

Approximate Time

30 to 40 minutes for activity (at home or in class)
15 minutes for discussion

Classroom Organization

Individuals, followed by whole-class discussion

Doing the Activity

Have students read the instructions in the student book carefully.

Discussing and Debriefing the Activity

You may want to have students share their cover letters as a way to start a summary discussion of the unit. Then let them brainstorm ideas of what they have learned in this unit. This is a good opportunity to review terminology and to place this unit in a broader mathematics context.

Blackline Masters

The Arithmetic of Graphs

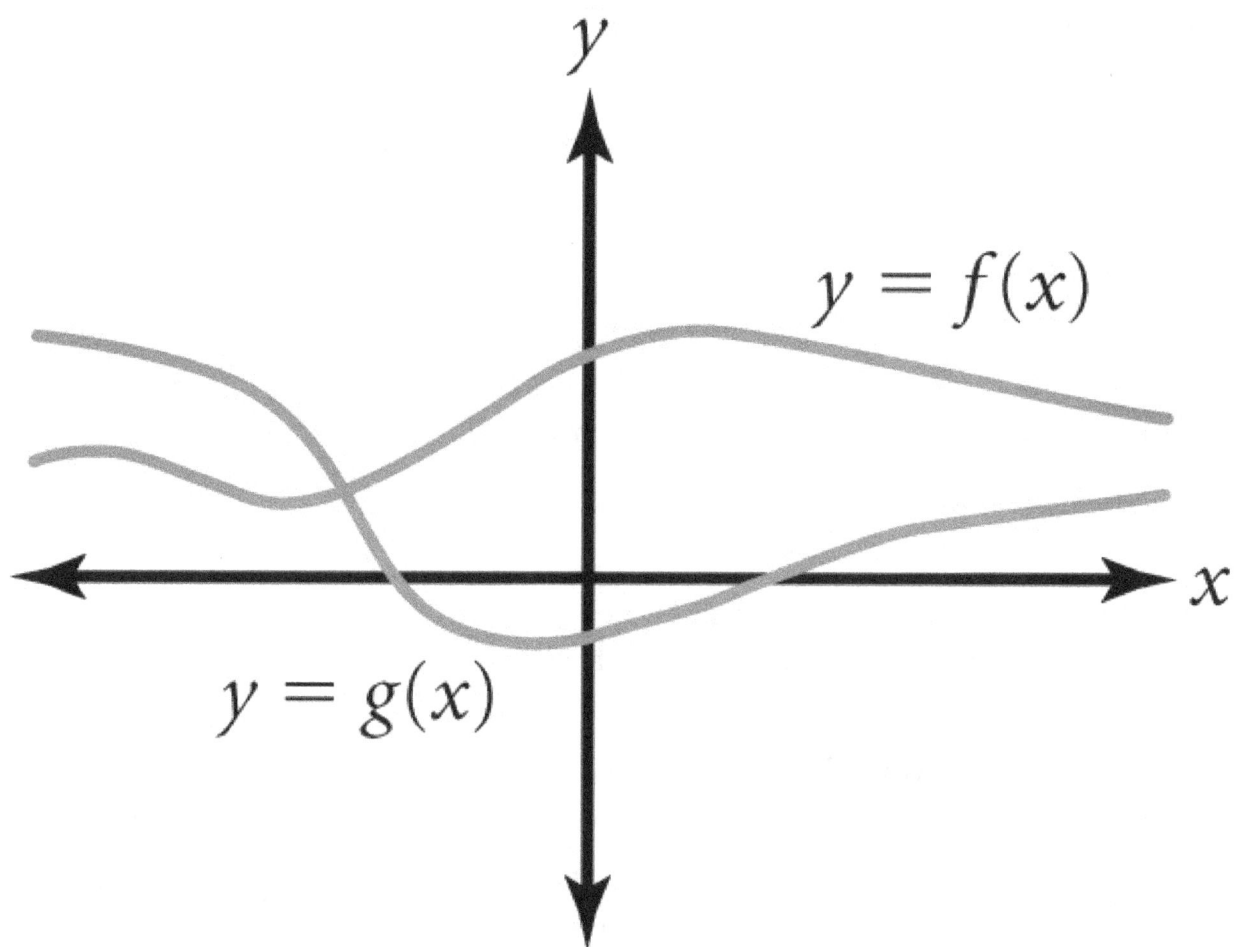

$$y = f(x)$$

$$y = g(x)$$

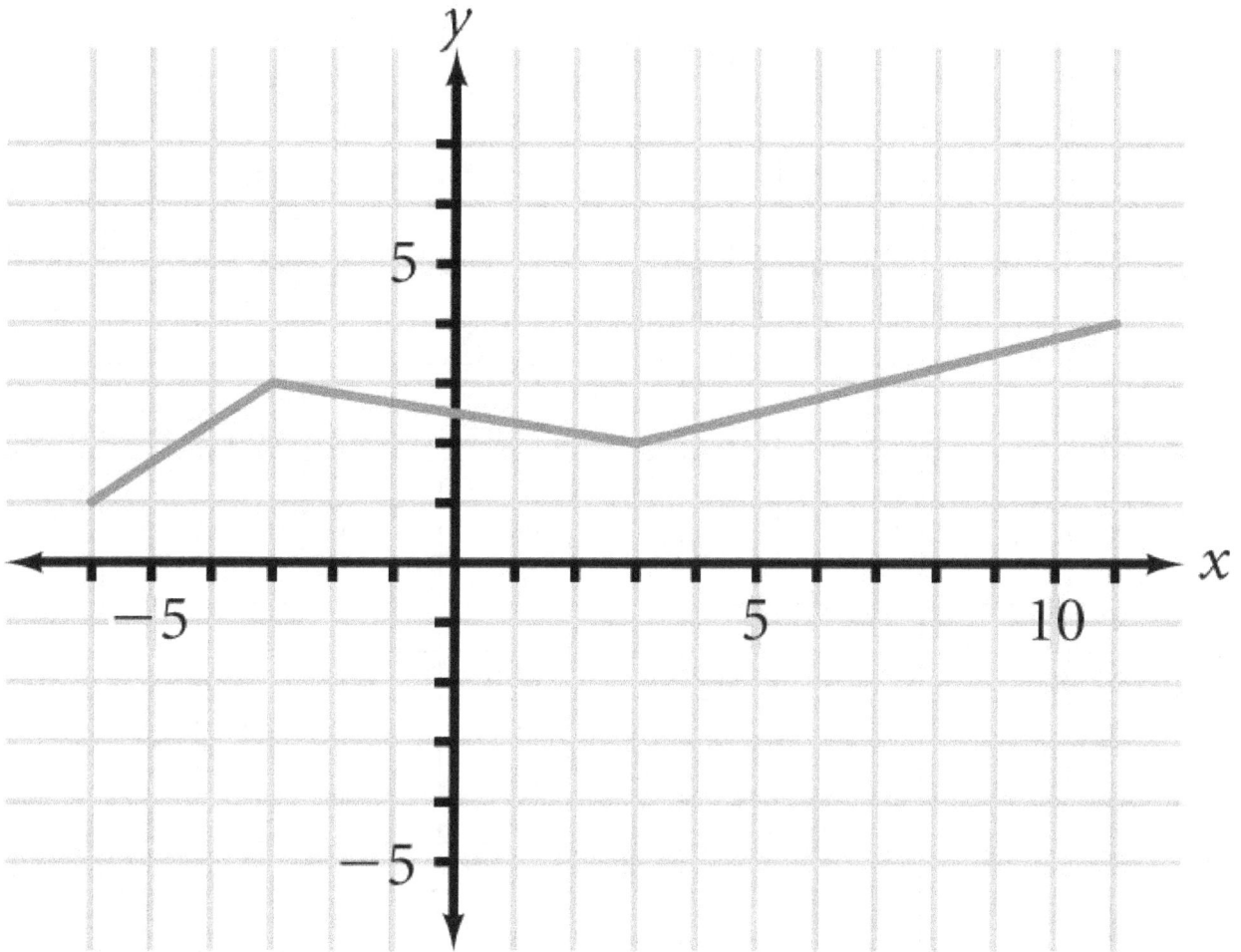

¼-Inch Graph Paper

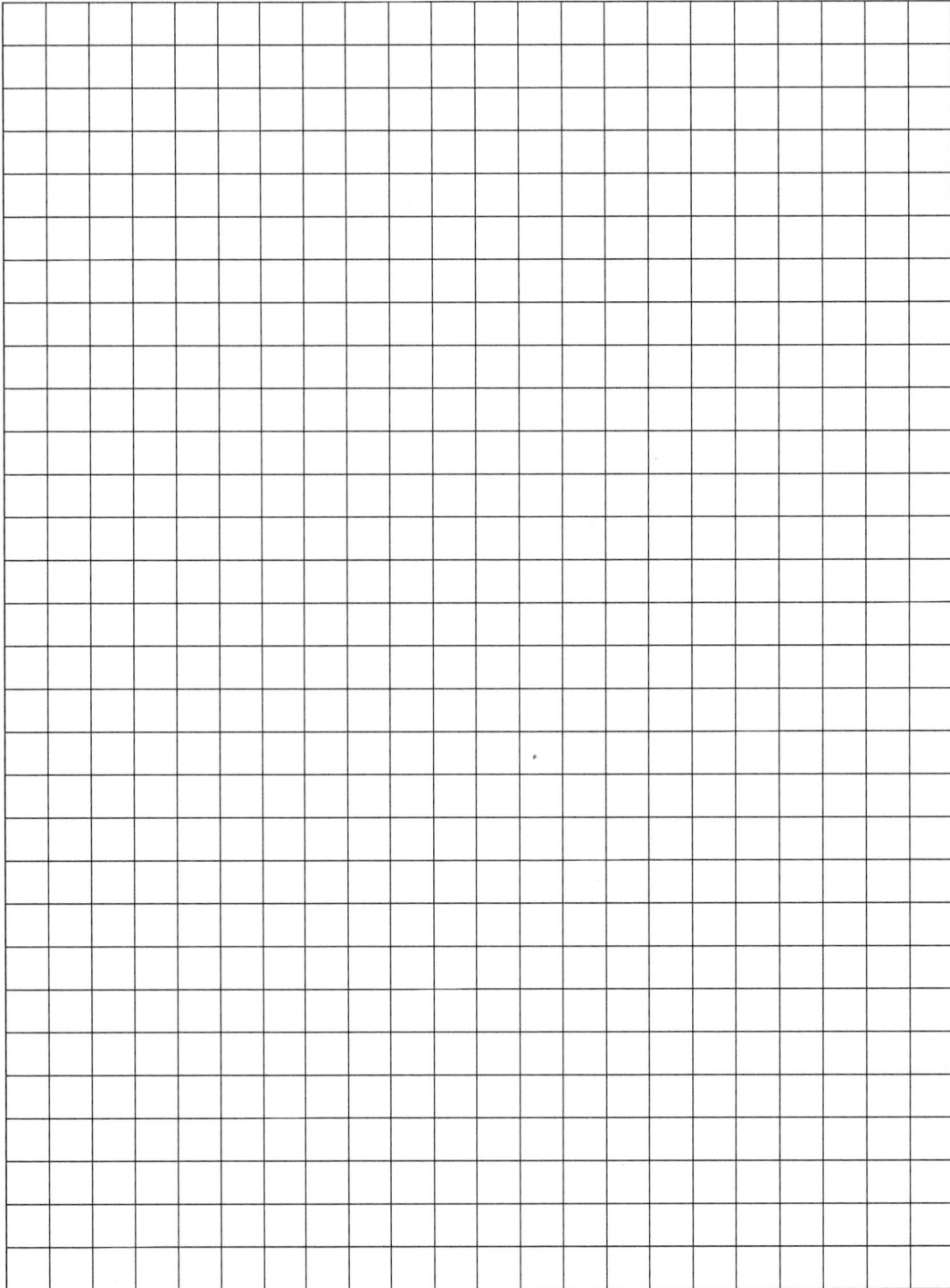

1-Centimeter Graph Paper

1-Inch Graph Paper

Assessments

In-Class Assessment

The chart gives *In-Out* tables for four functions, all using the same set of *x*-values.

Values in the table are either exact or have been rounded to the nearest 0.001. Your task is to find an algebraic equation for each of the four functions.

x	f(x)	g(x)	h(x)	k(x)
−5	−100	0.177	125	−0.1
−4.5	−90	0.210	101.25	−0.111
−4	−80	0.25	80	−0.125
−3.5	−70	0.297	61.25	−0.143
−3	−60	0.354	45	−0.167
−2.5	−50	0.420	31.25	−0.2
−2	−40	0.5	20	−0.25
−1.5	−30	0.595	11.25	−0.333
−1	−20	0.707	5	−0.5
−0.5	−10	0.841	1.25	−1
0	0	1	0	undefined
0.5	10	1.189	1.25	1
1	20	1.414	5	0.5
1.5	30	1.682	11.25	0.333
2	40	2	20	0.25
2.5	50	2.378	31.25	0.2
3	60	2.828	45	0.167
3.5	70	3.364	61.25	0.143
4	80	4	80	0.125
4.5	90	4.757	101.25	0.111
5	100	5.657	125	0.1

Part I: Guess My Graph

Read these four descriptions of situations in which one variable is a function of another.

Situation a: As shown here, three-fourths of a paper circle of radius r is used to form a cone. The paper is folded up so that the edges touch and the center of the circle becomes the bottom of the cone. The volume C of the cone is a function of r.

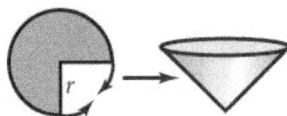

Situation b: An airplane flies from Milwaukee to Los Angeles at an average speed of s miles per hour. The time t required for the trip is a function of s.

Situation c: The tide is going in and out along the shoreline. The area A of the beach that is not covered by water changes as a function of t, the time elapsed since a certain starting point.

Situation d: A space probe traveling in a straight path at a constant speed flies past a small planet. For simplicity, assume the planet's position does not change. The distance d between the space probe and the planet is a function of t, the time elapsed from a given starting point.

The six graphs on the next page, U to Z, include graphs corresponding to the four situations described above.

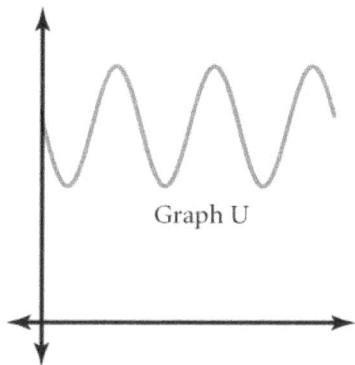

Graph U

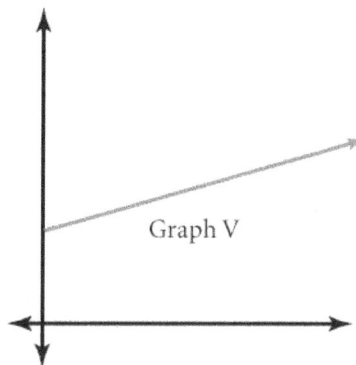

Graph V

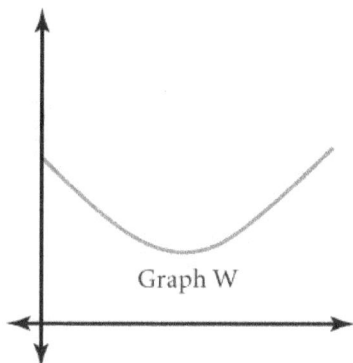

Graph W

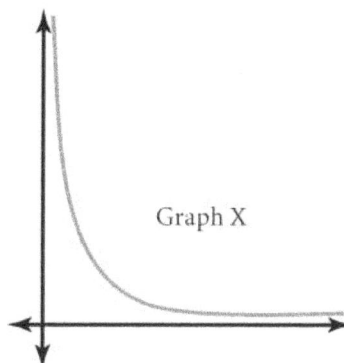

Graph X

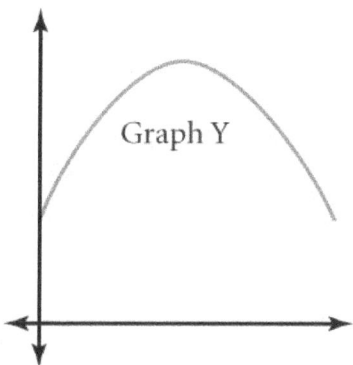

Graph Y

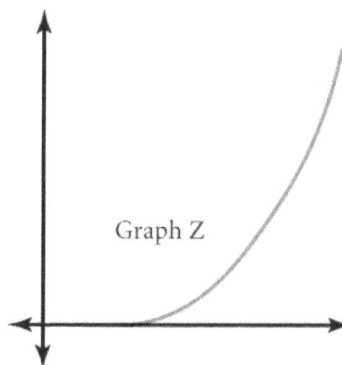

Graph Z

For each of situations a to d, do these things:

- State what function family you would use to represent the situation, and explain your reasoning.

- State which of the six graphs you would use to represent the situation, and explain your reasoning.

Part II: Fill in the Table

This graph is for the function f defined by an equation $y = f(x)$.

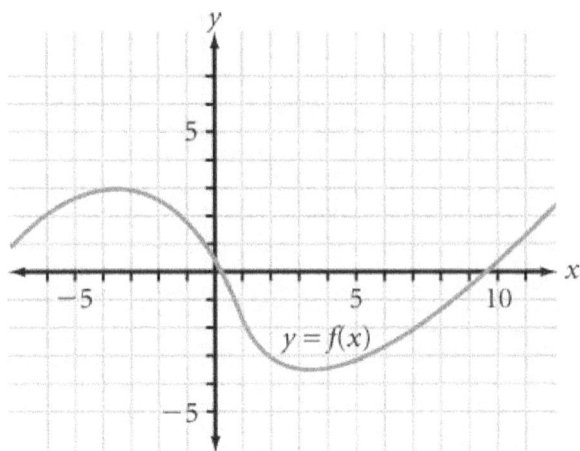

This table is for a function g.

x	g(x)
–5	3
–4	7
–3	8
–2	6
–1	3
0	0
1	–2
2	–1
3	2
4	5
5	9

Use the information in the graph for *f* and the table for *g* to fill in approximate values for each of the combined functions listed here.

x	*(f + g)(x)*	*(f · g)(x)*	*f(x + 2)*	*2g(x) + 1*
−5				
−3				
1				
3				
5				

I. The Diver Returns

1. Mike plays the tuba. His college's marching band is performing at halftime. At one point in the performance, the band members form a 100-foot-diameter circle in the center of the field. As the band begins to march around the circle, Mike is at the end of the circle closest to the goal line, which is 100 feet away. How far from the same goal line will he be after he has marched 320 degrees around the circle?

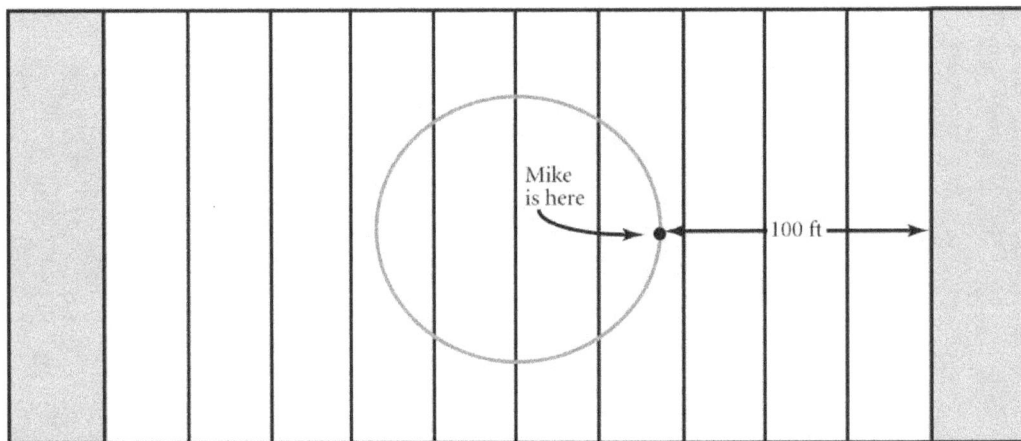

2. A coin is thrown downward with an initial velocity of 5 feet per second at an angle of 37° below the horizontal.

   a. How far will the coin move horizontally in the first 3 seconds?

   b. How far will the coin fall vertically in the first 3 seconds?

II. The World of Functions

1. a. Sketch the graph of a function that has both of these properties:

    - As x becomes very large in the positive direction, y becomes very large in the positive direction.
    - As x becomes very large in the negative direction, the graph has the x-axis as an asymptote.

   b. What is a possible algebraic equation that describes a graph like this? Explain.

2. The table shows the outputs for a function f for a given set of input values.

x	$f(x)$
−3	3
−2	0
−1	−1
0	0
1	3
2	8
3	15

   a. Plot the points represented by this table.

   b. Decide what family you think the function belongs to, and explain your reasoning.

   c. Find an algebraic expression for f that fits the information in the table.

III. The Pollster's Dilemma

1. You are one of two candidates running for office. Eighty percent of the population plans to vote for you. Of course, being humble, you have no idea that 0.8 is the true proportion. Though everyone keeps telling you that you will win, you don't quite believe it.

   When a 7-person poll is conducted, you say that you will eat your hat if five or more of the respondents plan to vote for you. What is the probability that you will be glad you have a very small hat size—that is, that five or more will say they plan to vote for you?

2. A driver's license test has a mean score of 63 with a standard deviation of 15. If 75 is the minimal passing score, about what percentage of people who take the test will pass?

The World of Functions Calculator Guide for the TI-83/84 Family of Calculators

Although the activities in this unit require much graphing by hand, the unit also makes heavy use of the graphing calculator. The calculator's table and function graphing capabilities, encountered in earlier units, are revisited. Student's blind faith in calculator graphs may be shaken a bit by consideration of the calculator's treatment of asymptotes. The unit also considers the plotting of data sets on the calculator, which most students will have seen in previous years of the IMP curriculum. Finally, the unit explores the use of the calculator's powerful regression capabilities. Students will learn that there is more to finding an appropriate function to fit a data set than simply telling the calculator to run a regression.

Brake!: When confronted in this activity with the problem of making a prediction based on a table of data, some students will undoubtedly remember using a curve-fitting process on the calculator in the Year 1 units *The Pit and the Pendulum* and *The Overland Trail.* While it will not be a problem if some students pursue this approach today, don't let the entire class get started down that path. Students will be better introduced to the work of the next two weeks by drawing graphs on paper and by looking for patterns within the tabulated data set. (In fact, this activity requests that students do both of these things.) You might suggest to students who immediately begin to try to plot the data set on the calculator that they first complete the initial two parts of the problem on paper.

Instructions for plotting data sets on a calculator graph are presented in the Calculator Note "Plotting Data on the Calculator," intended for use following *The Decision About Dunkalot.* It is probably not worthwhile to spend class time reviewing those procedures at this time.

Linear Tables: Encourage students to use the TABLE feature of their calculators while working on this activity. Instructions for the TABLE feature can be found in the *High Dive* Calculator Note "Creating Tables on the Calculator." The basic steps are reviewed briefly here:

X	Y₁	
0	7	
5	27	
10	47	
15	67	
20	87	
25	107	
30	127	

X=0

- Press Y= and enter the function.

- Define the parameters for the table by pressing 2ND [TBLSET]. **TblStart** defines the first input value for the table. **ΔTbl** is the spacing between input values of the table. Set **Indpnt** and **Depend** to **Auto** to generate a table automatically in accordance with **TblStart** and **ΔTbl**.

- Press 2ND [TABLE] to view the table.

Quadratic Tables: If students did not use the calculator's TABLE feature for *Linear Tables,* encourage them to do so for this activity. As the functions for the related activities become more complex over the next few days, use the TABLE feature to generate tables and to save time that is better spent in analyzing the tables.

Exponential Tables: This activity requires students to evaluate exponential functions. Exponents are entered on the calculator using the ^ key. For example, $y = 2^{3x}$ would be entered as **Y₁=2^(3X)**.

"Brake!" Revisited: Some students may have approached the *Brake!* by plotting the data set on the calculator and using a curve-fitting procedure similar to that used for the unit problem in the Year 1 unit *The Pit and the Pendulum.* Suggest that students not use such an approach for *"Brake!" Revisited,* but instead focus on what they now know about the families of functions and how they can use that to find a formula.

Don't Divide That!: As mentioned in the *Teacher's Guide,* remind students that they should graph the functions in this activity by hand before graphing them on the calculator. Though the calculator graph for the second function may surprise students, the mechanics of graphing these functions should not give them difficulty. If some students are less familiar with calculator graphing, you might provide them with a copy of the Year 3 *High Dive* Calculator Note "Graphing Functions."

A few students may need to be reminded to use parentheses when entering the function $y = \dfrac{10}{3 - x}$ into their calculators.

The End of the Function: During the discussion of end behavior of functions, students are asked to trace the graph of $f(x) = \left(1 + \dfrac{1}{x}\right)^2$. This is performed by displaying the graph on the graphics screen and then pressing the left- or right-arrow. Use the arrows to move the cursor along the graph of the function. If the coordinates of the cursor are not displayed at the bottom of the screen, **CoordOn** must be selected from the window format menu; this is found by pressing 2ND [FORMAT].

The Decision About Dunkalot: The *Teacher's Guide* suggests that prior to discussing this activity, you compare the two functions to the data set on the graphing calculator. The Calculator Note "Plotting Data on the Calculator" presents detailed instructions for accomplishing this.

The Calculator Note "Regression on the Calculator" will be useful during the discussion of regression, which is detailed in the *Teacher's Guide.*

Midnight Express: Students may ask how the graphs from this activity could be displayed on the calculator. For Question 1, select the absolute value function from the **NUM** menu under the MATH key. It appears there as the first menu item, **abs(**.

For Question 2, the greatest integer function is found as **int** under the MATH **NUM** menu. See the discussion in the *Teacher's Guide* concerning the limitations of the greatest integer function for representing this problem situation.

The Cost of Pollution: The *Teacher's Guide* includes discussion of a calculator analogy to composition. Details of this procedure are found in the Year 3 *High Dive* Calculator Note "Graphing a Complicated Function."

Plotting Data on the Calculator

These instructions use the following data set from *The Decision About Dunkalot* to review the procedure for plotting a data set on the calculator and comparing it to a function.

Day	Strength
1	55
6	90
13	140
18	185

1. Press Y= and either clear each function or make it inactive. (A function is active if the equal sign is highlighted. To make an active function inactive, move the cursor to the equal sign and press ENTER.)

2. Clear List 1 and List 2. To do this, press STAT and then press ENTER to select **Edit**. You will see a screen similar to the one shown here, which may or may not have data items in the lists. If data items are displayed, use the arrow keys to move the cursor onto the **L1** heading, as shown. Press CLEAR ENTER to clear the entire list. Move the cursor to the **L2** heading and press CLEAR ENTER to clear that list as well.

3. Enter the data items from the table into List 1 and List 2. To do this, move the cursor back to the first position beneath the **L1** heading. As you enter each data item from the input side of the table, it will be displayed initially at the bottom of the screen. Pressing ENTER after each data entry will cause that piece of data to be inserted into List 1. After you enter the input side of the table, move the cursor to the first position in List 2 and enter the output side of the table in the same way.

4. Turn on the plotting feature. Press 2ND [STAT PLOT] and then press ENTER to select **Plot1**. A screen similar to that shown here will appear. Carry out these steps:

    a. Press ENTER to select **On**.

    b. Move the cursor to the first symbol for graph type (scatter graph) and press ENTER.

    c. Select **L1** for the **Xlist**. This is done by positioning the cursor after **Xlist** and pressing 2ND [L1]. ([L1] is located above the 1 key.)

    d. Select **L2** for the **Ylist** in a similar manner.

    e. Select a mark to use for plotting your data set. The box-shaped mark is particularly easy to see on the graph screen.

5. Set your viewing window. The quickest way to define a viewing window that is just large enough to display all of the data points from the table is to press ZOOM 9 to select **ZoomStat**. Of course, the viewing window can also be defined or adjusted by pressing WINDOW and setting **Xmin**, **Xmax, Ymin,** and **Ymax** to encompass the minimum and maximum values from Lists 1 and 2.

    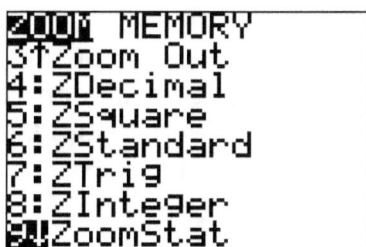

6. Enter the functions at Y= that are to be compared to the plotted data. If more than one function is being graphed at a time, you can select a heavier line for one of the functions. Move the cursor to the line symbol in front of the function and press ENTER to select the heavier line.

7. Press GRAPH to view the functions and plotted data items together.

Regression on the Calculator

These instructions assume that you have already entered the coordinates for the points into Lists 1 and 2 at the STAT **Edit** screen.

1. Press STAT and then use the right arrow to display the **CALC** menu. Press the appropriate number key to select the desired regression option. For a linear regression, select **LinReg(ax+b)**. Notice that the calculator provides options for several other types of regression. The choice of a particular regression should be based on some reason that the particular family of functions makes sense with the problem situation or data set.

```
EDIT CALC TESTS
1:1-Var Stats
2:2-Var Stats
3:Med-Med
4 LinReg(ax+b)
5:QuadReg
6:CubicReg
7↓QuartReg
```

2. Step 1 will cause the regression command to appear on the home screen. Press ENTER to perform the regression.

```
LinReg(ax+b)
```

3. The results of the regression will be displayed. The first part of the display will show the general function, with variables for the coefficients. Below that will be the values for each of those coefficients. The calculator does not display the correlation coefficient by default, but there are two ways to access this value.

   a. To find the correlation coefficient for a regression that has just been performed, press VARS, press 5 to select **Statistics**, use the right arrow to display the **EQ** menu, and then press 7 to copy **r** onto the home screen. Press ENTER to display the value of r.

   b. To cause the calculator to display the correlation coefficient on future regression calculations, from the home screen press 2ND [CATALOG] (above the 0 key) and use the down arrow to scroll to **DiagnosticOn**. Press ENTER once to copy this command to the home screen, and then press ENTER once more to execute it. If a regression is performed as described in Steps 1 and 2, the calculator will now display both r and r^2, known as the coefficient of determination.

```
CATALOG          ▯
 Degree
 DelVar
 DependAsk
 DependAuto
 det(
 DiagnosticOff
▶DiagnosticOn
```

4. The results of the regression can be pasted directly onto the [Y=] screen for graphing. Press [Y=] and position the cursor in the location you'd like to paste the equation. Press [VARS] and then [5] to select **Statistics**. Use the right arrow to display the **EQ** menu. Select **RegEQ** and press [ENTER]. The equation will be inserted at the [Y=] screen.

```
Plot1 Plot2 Plot3
\Y1■7.5739644970
414X+45.54733727
8107
\Y2=
\Y3=
\Y4=
\Y5=
```

www.ingramcontent.com/pod-product-compliance
Lightning Source LLC
LaVergne TN
LVHW081315060426
835509LV00015B/1524